CREATIVE SELLING

The world's greatest
life insurance salesman
answers your questions
about

CREATIVE SELLING

Ben Feldman

FARNSWORTH PUBLISHING COMPANY, INC.
ROCKVILLE CENTRE, NEW YORK

May I dedicate this book to Fritzie—my
own beautiful brown-eyed Fritzie—for
being with me—for listening to my problems—for always giving me something to
hold on to—for helping me help others
and for always being there when I needed
someone there . . . I'm grateful . . . .

—Ben

FOREWORD

Someone once remarked that if Ben Feldman didn't exist, he would have to have been "invented."

Thirty two years ago as I left the Pittsburgh area for Home Office Assignment I met Ben Feldman as he was beginning his extraordinary career! So it has been a special privilege to watch Ben's growth at close hand and see him achieve the reputation for being the man who "raised the sales sights of an industry."

Any man who has, single-handedly, put more than $600,000,000 on the life insurance books in a little over 30 years has certainly earned the title of the country's most creative and hard-working agent. Who else then could be better qualified to write about creative salesmanship than Ben Feldman?

Today the million-dollar case has become rather routine in various home office underwriting departments—thanks to Ben's utterly contagious ability to think BIG! Today multi-million insurance proposals no longer raise eyebrows because Ben sought out big answers to big problems—because Ben thrives on multi-million-dollar challenges.

And throughout it all Ben has remained humble and in low key. And what does Ben worry about most? The big cases that get away! Not because of a lost commission, but because Ben knows that a big problem, unsolved, is still there. Somehow he feels the man with the big problem was "a better salesman than I was." Unsolved problems have always bothered Ben.

This book is typical of Ben's desire to share his philosophy and his methods with all who'll listen. How fortunate we are to be in the life insurance business at a time when we can take such tremendous inspiration from that gifted high school "drop-out" who has gone on to become a legend in his own time.

DUDLEY DOWELL
(Retired, President
New York Life Insurance Company)

October, 1973

Contents

Contents

Contents

Contents

Contents

About the Author

Ben Feldman is generally acknowledged to be the world's greatest life insurance salesman and one of the nation's all-time great salesmen in any field.[1] After giving up a $10 a week job as an egg peddler for his father, he began his career in life insurance as a debit salesman in 1938. Three years later he joined his present company (New York Life) and in 1944, at the urging of his Manager, he concentrated on selling business insurance. This was the beginning of his meteoric rise to the zenith of success in both earnings and accomplishments, beyond doubt the most remarkable career in the history of life insurance selling.

Ben Feldman has written individual life insurance coverages totaling more than $850,000,000. He has an annual average of about $22,000,000 in coverage over a quarter of a century and in a single year has sold as much as $100,000,000.

Feldman's sales methods were the subject of a best-selling book by his former Manager, Andy Thomson.[2] Creative Selling, by Ben Feldman, represents a reinforcement and extension of his sales methods. Its format -- answers to questions about his philosophy and selling methods -- is a natural one for Ben since the questions are selected from those he's asked most frequently in platform appearances throughout the nation and abroad.

---

[1] B.C. Forbes, *America's Twelve Master Salesmen* (B.C. Forbes, 1952); Edwin P. Hoyt, *The Supersalesmen* (World Publishing Co., 1962); Perrin Stryker, *The Incomparable Salesmen* (McGraw Hill, 1967).

[2] Andrew H. Thomson, *The Feldman Method* (Farnsworth Publishing Co., Inc., 1969).

PART 1

PART I

1

DON'T SELL LIFE INSURANCE— SELL WHAT LIFE INSURANCE CAN DO . . .

*Can you give me an example
of what you mean by that, Ben?*

I had a case—an astute business man. Know what he was worth? *Millions.* Know how much insurance he had? Practically none. Only $2,000. He became successful by making his dollars work real hard. And what's a hardworking dollar? A dollar that brings in a big return. That's why he was a millionaire—he didn't want to use his dollars in any *other* way. He thought, why should he put his dollars in insurance when they could be working much harder in his own business? He didn't want to stop growing and he needed all the dollars he had.

But you know something? As he grew he needed more dollars. And one day he ran out of dollars. He had all those wonderful investment opportunities but he had no dollars to invest; all his dollars were tied up in other investments.

What did he do? What would *you* have done? He did exactly that: he went down to the bank to borrow some money. A *lot* of money. This man was a big investor. He needed big money. Is a million dollars big money? That's what this man went to the bank and asked for—a million dollars.

The banker said to him: "A million dollars? Well, that's a lot of money. Sure, we know you, and we know all about your success, and we know you'll make a lot of progress with that million dollars. But a million dollars! How long do you think it'll take you to pay it back?"

"Well," this man said, "I've worked out a projection." He showed the banker a sheet with a lot of figures on it. "Here are my investments, and here's what I can figure these investments will return me per year, and here's how long I can project it's going to take me to pay you back."

And how long was that? A good many years. It would be years and years before the bank would get its million dollars back.

The banker said to him: "How do we know you have that time? Suppose you run out of time—what happens to our money?"

And you know something? The banker was right. If something happened to the man, what would happen to the bank's money? And something *could* happen. Tell me, do you know anyone who has a lease on life? No one has a lease on life. The banker wanted to know that in case this man died before he paid back the million dollars, the bank could still get back the million dollars.

So the banker said to him: "How much insurance do you have?"

The man had to admit that he didn't have much insurance.

"What's it amount to?" the banker said.

"Practically nothing."

"Practically nothing!" the banker said—and he didn't sound at all like a friendly banker. "You mean to tell me you want us to put a value on your time of *one million dollars,* but the value *you yourself* put on your time is practically nothing! We just can't do it."

The banker turned him down. Tell me, had the banker done anything else, wouldn't he have been out of his mind?

Now, what did my man need to get that loan? Life insurance? Yes. But what did he really need—deep down? We're going back to basics, to fundamentals. What did he really need to get the money from the bank? What the man needed was *time*. Time to complete his plans. Time to pay back the million dollars. But he *couldn't guarantee* that he'd have the time—so what was he to do?

What the bank wanted was a guarantee that if the man ran out of time, the day he walked out, a million dollars would walk in. And *when* could he run out of time? *Any*time. Tomorrow. The next day. Does anyone know when time runs out? That million dollars had to be created *now*—ready to walk in *any*time. And what can create a million dollars that fast? Life insurance. Nothing but life insurance.

So this man—who had refused to see me when I first began to call on him—said to me:

"Ben, I still don't need life insurance—but I sure can use what life insurance can do for me."

And what could life insurance *do* for him? He needed time to accumulate the money to pay back the loan. Life insurance guaranteed the money in case he ran out of time. *What did life insurance do for him? It underwrote time. Time to complete his plans. Time to do what had to be done.*

And isn't that the same with *every* man? All men die someday. Never at the right time. Always at the wrong time. They didn't have quite enough time to complete their plans, make their dreams come true—and that's why it's always the wrong time. Who'll give them *more* time? Only The Man Upstairs. But we can give them the equivalent of time—in the sense that we give them the money to complete their plans. You know, we sell contracts for time and money. We can't guarantee the time—but we *can* guarantee the money.

2

THE BASIC PURPOSE OF LIFE INSURANCE IS TO CREATE CASH

*Exactly how does
life insurance buy time?*

Pick up a policy. Read the front page again. What does it say? "We promise to pay." Pay *what*? "The face amount." *When*? "Immediately in case of death." Tell me, when will that be? It could be anytime. When that time comes, we walk in with—*what*? "The face amount." Cash that *guarantees* that a man can raise his family, continue his business, pay off his home, educate his children, secure his wife's

7

welfare, complete all he's ever dreamed of doing—*even though he's no longer there*! "The face amount." With a drop of ink, a piece of paper and a few pennies we create *instantly* what a man had hoped to accumulate *eventually*. How does life insurance buy time? By *creating* money. What else but life insurance can *create* money?

When a man buys an insurance policy we put the face amount in escrow. That amount wasn't accumulated. It was created *for* the policyholder. You know, most men get their money by accumulating it—accumulating it slowly, painfully over the years. But our job is not to accumulate. Our job is to create. *What do we create? Dollars that underwrite time.*

The basic purpose of life insurance is to create cash: Nothing more, nothing less. Everything else just confuses. Your job is to do what no one else can do. Do you know anyone else who can *create money*?

You know what I carry in my case? A thousand dollar bill. I'll walk up and open my case, and the prospect will look at the thousand dollar bill, and he'll say, "What's *that*?" And I'll say, pointing to the thousand dollar bill:

"That's what I sell. This thousand dollar bill comes in packages of a hundred. How many do you want?"

You can see the wonderful thing that you're selling: contracts for delivery of money.

3

LIFE INSURANCE CREATES CASH AT A DISCOUNT WHEN A MAN NEEDS IT MOST

*I've often heard you say you
deliver "discounted dollars."
What do you mean by that, Ben?*

Sometimes I say to a man: "Give me three cents and I'll give you a dollar. I'll put that dollar in escrow. I'll write your name on it. I'll keep it in escrow for a year. If anything happens to you, we'll trade: I'll keep the three cents and you get the dollar. And at the end of the year, if nothing happens to you, I'll repeat the offer. One dollar for another year for three cents!"

And I'll repeat the offer year after year.

At three cents a year, it takes a long time to pay a dollar for a dollar, doesn't it? You know what kind of dollars you're buying? You're buying *discounted dollars*.

The three cents I talked about? That's the premium. For a man in his early forties, the premium is about thirty dollars per thousand—and that's about three cents per dollar.

The premiums go up the older a man gets. For a man in his fifties, I've got a dollar I'll sell for a nickel. For a man in his sixties, I've got a dollar I'll sell for six cents.

Look at the life expectancy tables: the odds are a man will never pay in as much as we pay out. So the dollars we provide almost always come to a man at a discount. We don't only provide a man with the dollars he needs to complete his plans—we provide those dollars at a discount.

Do you see this wonderful thing the insurance industry has done? Look at it this way: The insurance industry has designed a machine—a money-making machine —and it makes discounted dollars.

And when does it deliver those discounted dollars? *Exactly* when a man needs them; when time has run out, when there is no more time for him to complete his plans. Discounted dollars—to take the place of the time he no longer has. Discounted dollars—to make everything he wanted to come true, come true.

These discounted dollars are tax-free. I say to a man, "Here's an option on a dollar for one year at three cents. I guarantee the dollar. And when you pick up the option, your dollar is tax-free."

Go in and tell your prospect what you're selling are contracts that *guarantee* the delivery of tax-free dollars at a discount. Insurance is the closest thing to getting something for nothing I've ever found.

4

SELL TAILORED DOLLARS

*What do you mean when you say
the discounted dollars you sell are tailored?*

Remember the business man I talked about who needed a loan from the bank? He wouldn't see me, he wouldn't let me in the door, until he had a *specific* problem. What was it? A million dollars worth of credit. He didn't want life insurance, but he did want what life insurance would do for him—get him the credit he needed.

I'd say to this man: "Mr. Jones, you have a credit

problem. A million dollars. May I show you my idea? The day
you walk out, a million tax-free dollars walk in. And you
only pay a small fraction of that million dollars." Tailored
dollars to insure a credit line!

My work is to make the policies fit. You know,
when you buy a pair of pants or a pair of shoes, you just can't
buy any pair. You make sure they fit. Like a tailor with a
bolt of cloth, I make life insurance fit. That's what I mean
when I say I sell life insurance as tailored dollars.

*Can you give me another
example of tailored dollars
—discounted dollars that help
solve a man's specific problem?*

How about a man who leaves an estate? You know,
if the estate is any real size, Uncle Sam can take a third of it.
They call it taxes.

Say to this man: "Mr. Jones, you have a problem.
No one has a lease on life and most men never die at the right
time; there is no right time. Mr. Jones, the taxes must be
paid *from* your estate—or *for* your estate. Let me pay it *for*
your estate—with discounted dollars." Those are tailored
dollars to pay estate taxes.

And there are so many, so many other specific
problems that tailored dollars can solve.

5

PINPOINT
A MAN'S
PROBLEM

*Can you show me how
you pinpoint a man's problem?*

Tailored dollars help a man solve a specific problem.
So one of the keys to selling is simply to look for the problem.
If I could find a problem that's going to cost you or your
family money, you need insurance. Make *sure* that you *have*
found the problem, that you recognize it, that you understand
it so well that you know the price of doing something about it,
and the price of doing nothing about it. I will show you that

by doing nothing, it will cost you dollars, but by doing
something, it will cost you pennies.

So find the problem. Pinpoint a man's problem.
Explain to the man that there's *a price tag* on doing something, and there's *a price tag* on doing nothing. The price
tag on doing nothing is a lot higher in the end.

Here's an example. I say to a man:

"You spent thirty years putting this company together. I've never known anybody who had a lease on life, do
you? No? Then it's only a question of time until you walk out
and Uncle Sam walks in. Know what he wants? Money! And
he has a way of getting it. First. Not last. Could you, right
now, give me 30 percent of everything you own—in cash?
That's the least Uncle Sam will take. Could you give it to me
without it hurting a little bit?

"You spend a lifetime locking money up in bricks
and stone and steel. Someday, someone will have to unlock
those bricks and convert them back into money. Wouldn't
it be easier to hire me for $10 a day and let me do this for
you? The day you walk out, $100,000 walks in."

6

THE PROBLEM MUST HAVE A PRICE TAG

*Will you give me another
demonstration of how you
sell by pinpointing a problem
with a price tag?*

I might say something like this:

"You spend a lifetime making money, plowing it back into a successful corporation, becoming quite wealthy, worth a lot of money—and yet you have no money. That is, money in the form of dollars. To keep growing, you converted dollars into other assets. In other words, you locked them up.

17

"But someday, you're going to have to *unlock* them. And if you're not here, that may become a liquidation. The other word for liquidation is quite often—loss. You spend a lifetime accumulating assets; someone will take them apart over night. You're going to need some dollars and I have dollars that are guaranteed and discounted. They cost pennies a piece. You never pay in the amount you pay out. Furthermore, your gain is free of income tax. You're going to need money. Why can't you use my dollars? They cost pennies a piece!

"There's a price tag on everything. By doing nothing it will cost you dollars. By doing something it will cost you pennies."

7

CREATE
SPECIFIC IDEAS
FOR SPECIFIC
PROBLEMS

First, you start with a *problem*. The problem must have a price tag. Then you create *specific ideas* for *specific problems*. You know, ideas are the keys that unlock a case. Once the man has accepted the idea, he's bought the insurance. Show a man simple, easy-to-understand ideas which tell a man how you can solve his problem.

You're not selling insurance. You're selling ideas—ideas to solve a man's problems.

19

Ben, I assume that you have come up with many ideas for solving specific problems. Will I be able to use them when I sell?

There are so many good ideas—some mine, some from others—none completely original. You're welcome to use my ideas. If you work with them, they'll become *your* ideas.

If you can get just one idea that will work for you, one idea that can start you thinking bigger, then this book will have been worthwhile and you'll be on your way.

Perhaps an idea can start you thinking bigger and can raise your sights. You know, a man is only as big as he thinks he is. There's no limit to what you can do.

8

PACKAGE YOUR IDEAS

What do you mean when you say you "package" your ideas to solve a man's problem?

The key to a sale is the idea, and the key to selling the idea is to package it.

When I was just beginning to sell, I would say: "You want to be sure your daughter goes to college? May I show you this idea . . . ?" And what was the idea? It was an *education package*. It wasn't insurance this man wanted; he wanted his daughter to go to college. So I didn't talk about anything else. I showed him how we could guarantee that his daughter would go to college—and I used words and figures he was sure to understand. That was my package.

Or I would say to a man, "How would you like to retire with a guaranteed income for the rest of your life? Here's an idea I have. May I show it to you?" What he wanted was a guaranteed retirement income—*not* insurance. And I showed him how to get what he wanted. That's *all* I showed him. I made it very direct, very easy to understand. And that was my *retirement package*.

I had lots of packages for different purposes. I would say to a man, "I have a special package of money designed for people like you." Each package was different. I'd have each package worked out in my own head so I could talk about it clearly and a man could understand what I was talking about. I sold simple packages designed to help a man with his problem.

9

KEEP YOUR PACKAGES SIMPLE

When you started out, your packages were simple. Do you mean to say that now when you sell big-dollar packages, you can still keep your packages simple?

The key to packaging an idea is to make it simple. Insurance tends to be complex. I can't understand it unless it's simple. The simpler the better. When something is simple it's easier to sell than when something is complicated. To sell something, make it easy to understand—and you do that when you keep it simple.

23

You know something? I don't do anything different these days. I still sell packages. Do you know what I call myself? A package salesman. I create and sell simple clean-cut packages, each with a purpose, a single-minded purpose. The purpose is to solve a problem that's very serious —very real, very real. So a man *needs* and *must have* my package.

Ben, how did you get the idea of selling
life insurance in the form of simple packages?

One of the things I learned early was that you have to know what you're doing. So I would spend hour after hour with the rate book until I knew it inside out, upside down. There were all kinds of contracts in it, and I learned them. You see, the rate book, basically, is just mechanics—2 plus 2 makes 4. I had to make sure a policy didn't make 5; that it only made 4. I had to understand it, and I couldn't understand it unless I made it simple. So it became simple.

Then I could fit the prospect like a tailor would fit a suit from a bolt of cloth. I could create a simple package to solve his problem. I would give my packages names. They were nothing but blocks of whole life, but I'd call them: Special policy designed to educate your little boy. A special housewife policy. For partners: a see-saw policy; you know, if one gets off, the other falls off.

After making up one special little package, I'd make up a list of names and I'd begin making my calls. "Let me show you a package of money designed for you ... " I was making some sales—and the sun was shining. But after a while, you know what would happen? The package would get old. It was still good, but I would lose my enthusiasm. You know what I would do then? I would make up another little pack-age and I'd give it a new name. And I would make up another list, and I'd go out again calling.

Ben, you said your packages were really blocks of whole life. Are they still blocks of whole life? What I mean is: today, life in-surance companies are marketing many different products—mutual funds, for example. Exactly what kind of life insurance product do you package, Ben?

You hear a lot about various types of products that are marketed by life insurance companies. What are they? Mutual funds, variable life, many things designed to go the way the economy goes up, or down, or both. Well, you know if a man wants to make a lot of money, he must take a lot of risks. Tell me, what happened to the stock market in the last couple of years? It was up. Fine. Then it went down. Not so fine. That's *not* the kind of foundation I want for myself and my family, or for the people depending on me. I'd like to be sure when I'm gone that there's something *there*—a real foundation—something my people can depend on.

You know, many men spend a lifetime putting things together, and then see all they built up falling apart. A man's plans for his family, his business, the people he worked with—all falling apart. All his dreams—dreams which he built up slowly over the years brick by brick—all his dreams ending in a crash. So I think a man must build some-thing strong, solid, firm—guaranteed. He must ask, "Will what I'm building *on* keep all I've built *up* from falling apart?"

He must know that there will always be something *there* that's
absolutely dependable, so that when his family needs it, they'll
have it. I think you'll find when the chips are down, a man
will buy life insurance for its certainty—for the assurance
that what he built up *won't* fall apart.

Sometimes I say to a man, "Your life insurance is
so basic to the security of your family. The day you fall apart,
all you have *could* fall apart. Creditors come first, your family
comes second. But *not* if you build a personal program that
provides basic security to your family. You know, the policy
helps you protect your family against creditors in many ways.
In the State of Ohio there's even a 'spendthrift clause' in a
man's policy. Know what it does? It makes the proceeds of
the policy free from creditors' claims, so even if you were a
spendthrift your family would still be secure. Your family has
the right to go on living—and life insurance protects that right.
Let me show you how . . . "

There's no substitute for life insurance. There never
was and there never will be. There's no investment a man
could make that's anything like it. Why? What's the best
investment? The one that pays the most when it's needed
most. And, tell me, isn't that life insurance?

So what I sell is whole life. That's to secure the
future. And I sell term. That's an option on the future. And I
put these policies into packages.

10

SELL BIG PACKAGES

What's the difference between the packages you sell now and the packages you sold when you first started out?

They're bigger. All problems have price tags—some are simply bigger than others. My cases are bigger these days simply because the problems I solve have bigger price tags. When you create a package, make it big enough to do the job. Don't underestimate your prospect's needs.

27

Why did you start out with small packages?

I hadn't learned how to think big. Do you know how I started out selling insurance?

I lived in a little town, population about 1,500 people. The town was Salineville, Ohio, where my father set up a family business. My parents bought and sold produce, cattle, hogs, chickens, eggs, and it was a case of everybody pitching in and doing his part. We were by no means well-to-do. Our family was large, nine children, and my parents felt it important for me to chip in and carry the load. Dad paid me $5 per week. That was enough. I was living at home, and I didn't need any more money.

The years went by and some of the young kids were driving cars. I didn't have one. I sure wanted one, and I finally persuaded my Dad to give me a raise. He raised me to $10 a week, and the first thing I did was to go out and buy a new car. A Model-T Ford. I remember I was paying $25 a month for it. Since I was earning only $40 a month, it sure didn't give me much leeway to drive the car, but I did—and I finally got the car paid for. Well, you know what goes with a car?

Girls!

I knew one of the most gorgeous girls in the world. I began calling. And slowly, surely, time went by, and we wanted to get married. One day she really jarred me. She said that I couldn't support her on $10 a week. So, it seemed to me that I wasn't really needed at home, and I had better get myself a better paying job. Where do you look for a job in a little town of 1,500 people?

A friend of mine was working for an insurance company, and there just happened to be an opening. I knew he was earning $35 a week, which to me was a fabulous amount of money. I went down and applied for the job. The roof fell in. I didn't seem to measure up in any way, shape, or form. I was shy, I was backward, I talked with a lisp. I hadn't even finished high school. They tossed me out.

But a positive mental attitude, *that* more than anything else determines your success. If you decide you are going to feel wonderful, strong, excited—then you have the power to move mountains. I had this attitude. I never take "no" for an answer. If they throw me out one door, I'll come in another. So I came back, and I came back. And I finally got the job!

My friend was making $35 a week, but not me! I remember the very first week on the job, I wrecked my car. And when Saturday rolled around, I found I had earned $15 and couldn't get my car out of hock because the bill was *more* than $15.

I worked with this company on the debit. On a debit you're responsible primarily for collection, and I didn't like to collect. I wanted to call on people, to try to make sales. I would give the collection book to my assistant manager. He'd make my collection. I'd go calling. We'd meet at the end of the day, and by then I'd have some sales. My debit would grow. It got so big that one man couldn't handle it. So each year the company would cut it in half, and put another man on. This went on for three years. Until I got a chance to go with New York Life.

It was a big step. I wasn't quite sure I wanted to do it, and finally I did it on a trial basis. I was told, "Come on in and try it for 90 days, and if you don't like it, you can leave."

Meanwhile I got an expression from the debit company: "O.K., try it, but it won't work out. It just can't. At the end of 90 days come back."

I still wasn't sure I wanted to change jobs. Then the debit company said to me, "You'll never make good. You'll fall flat on your face. You shouldn't go at all. It's not for you."

And that did it! I decided I *would* make the change and I would *never* go back no matter what happened.

To answer your question, "Why did I start out with small packages?" Even when I got to New York Life, I was thinking debit size. I was thinking small.

What men helped you start thinking big?

When I started with New York Life, somehow I got the impression that it was normal to write 10 cases a week, and so I would report in on Friday afternoon, and I usually had my 10 cases. Oh, they weren't big. I was still thinking debit size.

At one of my very first meetings, Isaac Kibrick, that great salesman, was the guest of honor. In that particular month I had written 40 cases and I was so flattered when he singled me out for praise. My cases were small, but he said, "Your cases will grow. Some will become $10,000 cases, and some $25,000. Some, maybe $50,000. And some maybe even more."

The cases *did* grow. Why? The people grew, and I was tagging along, and as they grew, I grew.

There are so many, many men to whom I am indebted, and yet if I were to try and single out one, it would be Andy Thomson, formerly of our home office, because he, more than anyone else, gave me a track to run on. The track had to be simple or I couldn't stay on it. The track was three cases a week—just three cases a week.

"Pay no attention to the size of the case," Andy said. "The size of the case will grow as the years go by, as the people grow. You will grow in your thinking, your knowledge, your know-how."

You know, that's exactly what happened. Let me tell you about my first sale, as an example.

He was a boyhood friend of mine—from the same town. He wanted to buy a policy. I didn't know quite what he wanted or how to put it together. He wasn't quite sure of what he wanted either. He just wanted to buy the first policy that I'd write. So we both went down to the office manager and we put together a $5,000, 20-pay Life. I was really walking on the clouds!

As the years went by, this little case grew. I could see that each day this man was trading the day for the dollar, and he wrapped the dollar back into a growing expanding company. As his problems became bigger, his program became bigger. I had learned to "tag along behind your people, and as they grow, you'll grow." That's what happened in this little case. It grew and it grew and it grew. When I came to sell my first million-dollar policy, you know who I sold it to? *That* man, my first sale!

Remember, as time goes by, men grow—and as they grow, quite often their problems grow. The need is greater. So the solution must be greater.

What do you do different now when
you sell big policies than when
you sold small ones?

I'm not doing anything any different now than I was 20 years ago. If my package is big, it's because the man's problem has a big price tag. And you know something?— someday that price must be paid. It's true the prospect doesn't *have* to pay it. But if *he* doesn't pay it—and remember, we're talking about big price tags—price tags worth hundreds of thousands of dollars, sometimes millions—if *he* doesn't pay it, *his family* will *have* to pay it. And they'll have to pay it with *hundred-cent dollars*. Isn't it better for *him* to pay it since he can do so with *discounted dollars*?

Whether he buys my package or not, there's a price tag, either way—and *somebody* has to pay. Isn't it better for him to pay *pennies* instead of his family paying dollars? So even though the price tag is big, he pays very little for it. A man may need a half a million dollars, but he'll pay very little for that half a million dollars.

And when you show a man all that: when you show him the price tag is very real—when you show him that it must be paid—and when you show him that you can pay it *for* him *no matter how big it is*—and the cost to him will be pennies not dollars—then the man will see that he *needs* what you're presenting. You'll be on your way to a sale. A *big* sale.

11

TO SELL LARGER POLICIES— BUILD UP YOUR OWN PROGRAM

I confess I get a little tongue-tied when it comes to talking about big money. What can I do?

Years ago when I got started, I wrote $500 policies, and the reason they weren't smaller was: there wasn't anything smaller. And you know what was wrong? I didn't have much insurance. I think I had two thousand dollars worth. And most everyone I spoke to had *that*—or *more*. I was afraid of my prospects. Why? Because they were bigger than I was;

I was looking up at them. It's much harder to make a sale when you're looking up. It's very hard, very hard to make a sale when the man looks like a giant. He's got ten thousand dollars worth of insurance and I've got two thousand, and I'm telling *him* he should buy more. You know who should buy more? *I* should buy more.

So I began buying insurance for myself. I was starting out in life; I didn't have the money. At that time, I was buying insurance for which it seemed I couldn't pay. It's a funny thing: I had no money, but I *found* the money. And you know, you start out like that and then—a wonderful thing happens! *If you buy more, you sell more.* It's your clients who pay the premiums for *your* policies. *Do it*—you'll find it *will* work for you.

So I built up my program. And then I finally built myself up to where I had $50,000 worth of insurance—what happened? I found myself talking to a man with $100,000 worth of insurance. I had just $50,000! I was ashamed to have so little. In those days, if I were talking to a man who had $100,000 and I had $50,000, I would look up to him. He was bigger than I was, and I was scared.

So what did I do? I pulled myself up. But when I had $200,000, know what happened? There I was talking to somebody with $300,000. I was still afraid. So I continued increasing my personal program.

And you know, when you do, you feel *big*. When you have $500,000, and the man you're talking to has *only* $300,000—oh boy! You enjoy talking to that man.

And you know, when you raise your sights, you raise the other man's sights. And when you raise his sights you're helping him, because his problem has a big price tag, and only *you* can pay it for him. Isn't that a good thing?

So build your *own* insurance program. The best way to sell something is to first own it yourself. I'm not frightened to put up a proposal for a million dollar policy to any man.

As a rule, *you will sell each year ten times the amount of insurance you own. Build your own program up to one hundred thousand dollars, and you'll be writing one million dollars a year.*

Men grow, and if you stay with them you'll grow with them. Continue to study. Continue to build your own program.

12

HOW TO WRITE SIX MILLION DOLLARS IN THE NEXT SIX MONTHS

Don't be afraid to dream big dreams. They have a way of coming true. Strange as it seems, your biggest problem is to sell yourself. Most men exchange their lifetime for much too little. Don't be afraid to think big. Anything your mind can conceive, *that* you can achieve. Think small, and your cases will be small. Think big and your cases will be big.

If you want big volume, you have to look for men
with big price tags on their problems. How would you like
to write *six* million dollars in the next six months? Of course
you would. But you can't do it without big packages.

> *Even with big packages, Ben, six*
> *million dollars—that's an*
> *awful lot of money. You must have*
> *some secret—some special way*
> *of doing it. Have you?*

What you're saying is: Six million dollars! You
have to run so fast in six months, it doesn't look like it's
possible. It's too big. You think you can't do it.

But listen, and I'll tell you how to do it.

Take six million dollars and break it apart into
months: divide by six, and what have you got? One million
dollars a month. Still too big? All right, break it down some
more. How many weeks are there in a month? Four. Divide
one million by four. Now what have you got? $250,000 a
week. Now continue to break it down: break down that
$250,000 into three cases a week. Now you have less than
$100,000 a case. All you need is to write two or three cases
totaling $250,000 each week. If you miss today, know what?
You'll make it tomorrow.

Now it's do-able. You *can* do it. You can achieve
your goal. But you've got to start off with a goal—a *big* goal.
Why a *big* goal? You have to have a goal in the back of your
mind—let's call it a dream—big enough to be *exciting*. Because
unless it's exciting, it won't make you run. Six million dollars
in the next six months! *That's* exciting. That's something

big enough to get excited about. If it's not big enough to get excited about, you won't do it. So get a goal big enough to get excited about. Then make the goal do-able.

Start with a goal—a big goal that makes you excited. Then break it down into three cases a week. That's your deadline. You've got to run so far, so fast. Now you've got a track to run on. The key to the goal is the deadline. You must have goals and deadlines. One isn't good without the other. But together, they can be tremendous.

I started off years ago with a goal of three cases a week. When my cases got bigger, my volume got bigger.

Ben, what's the average size
of your case?

I think a year or so ago I had $54,000,000 on 139 cases. That averages out to about $388,000 a case.

13

TO FIND THE BIG CASE, FIND A MAN WITH A BIG PROBLEM

> *It's clear to me that if you're going to sell a case in six figures, you've got to find a man with a six-figure problem that life insurance can solve. What kind of problem is that?*

What you're really saying is, "Why are some cases bigger than others?"

The only difference is little problems and big problems. And where do you find the biggest problems? In estate tax situations, in close corporations, in partnerships. There are many packages to solve these kinds of problems.

How do you find a man with
these kinds of problems?

I'm driving down the road, and I see a sign over the door of a building: *The ABC Manufacturing Company.* It looks like a pretty sizeable operation.

Now the next thing I do is get a D&B report. That's a financial report on the ABC Company, which comes to you from Dun and Bradstreet, D&B. You can subscribe to their service. You can get a report, a D&B, on any company from them.

I've got the D&B—what do I do with it? I study it. I go over it very carefully. Now I know who owns the ABC Company. I find out it's a closely held corporation. The man who runs it is the man who owns it.

Now the next thing I look at is: What does he own? What does he owe? Does he have a lot of money or a lot of debts?

And I find out there isn't that much loose money floating around. This is a half-million-dollar business, but that half million dollars is locked up in brick and steel and land and machinery. All the money is in the business, not in cash.

What else do I know after reading this report?

Tell me, wouldn't it be logical to assume that the man owns a house, owns a car, that he's piled up certain investments, certain expensive possessions. So here's a man with an estate of maybe seven, eight hundred thousand dollars.

Then I know this: Uncle Sam wants two hundred thousand, three hundred thousand dollars from this man—that's the part of *his* estate that *isn't* his. So this man has a problem—a big problem—a problem with a big price tag.

"Mr. Jones, I have a package of money that will pay your estate taxes. With discounted dollars. Let me show it to you . . ."

Ben, I'd like to get back to the way you said you got started when you prospect for a big case. You said: you're driving down the road and you see a sign that says ABC Company or XYZ Company or whatever, and if it looks like a sizeable company, you look into it. Is that what you'd advise me to do?

Well, I do it, and it seems to work. But I tell you what you can do also. You can use a Directory—a Business Directory of your area, if there is one. You can go down the list and pick some companies that look large enough and get their D&Bs, and get started that way.

You know, I also get leads from reading the papers, and from an estate service I subscribe to, and from referrals.

Sometimes I know people who know a prospect. So I ask questions, discreet questions. And somewhere, someone may have written him a policy. I ask our Central Service Office, "Do we have any coverage on this man? If so, may I have a brief?"

When you're studying your D&B and sifting through all the other facts, look for problems in those three big price-tag areas—estates, close corporations, partnerships. And that's how you find the man with the big price-tag problems.

14

GET OUT
OF THE
OFFICE

When you've lined up your suspects,
how do you make contact with them?
Many agents I know put their feet
up on a desk and pick up the phone.

That's so wrong, so wrong. You're not selling when you're sitting in your office.

You know what I do sometimes after I've checked out my leads and suspect they have problems?

45

I make up a list of these suspects. Some of them I know *have* problems. So they're not suspects; they're prospects. I make up a list, and I take a month—not to make sales, but just to call on people. I'm going out to find people. But special people. People with problems. I'm taking time to say hello to people with problems.

Do you just go in cold?

I have, and I've seen many cold calls turn into sales. But what I do now is this: To that list of suspects and prospects I've worked up, I send this out on a monthly basis:

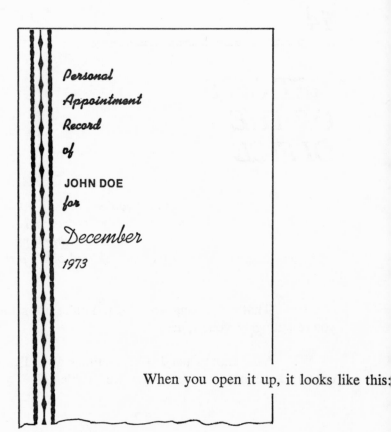

Personal

Appointment

Record

of

JOHN DOE

for

December

1973

When you open it up, it looks like this:

DECEMBER 1973

SUNDAY	MONDAY	TUESDAY	WEDNESDAY	THURSDAY	FRIDAY	SATURDAY
						1
2	3	4	5	6	7	8
9	10	11	12	13	14	15
16	17	18	19	20	21	22
23/30	24/31	25	26	27	28	29

THE DESKFINDER COMPANY · INDIVIDUALIZED ADVERTISING

2132 HARBOR BOULEVARD   COSTA MESA, CALIFORNIA 92627

47

It's very useful to help a man keep his appointments. Even the back is useful, because there's a scratchpad on it, and there's a place to mark down future appointments.

The man I call on gets these *Personal Appointment Records* month after month. He uses them, and he gets to know my name. I also send out letters from time to time—and there are a number of them in the book Andy Thomson wrote about me.*

So when I walk in and say to a secretary, "I'm Ben Feldman and I'd like to get acquainted with Mr. Jones," and the secretary picks up the intercom and says, "Mr. Jones, Mr. Feldman is here to see you," he'll know who Ben Feldman is. Maybe because he knows who I am, and because he wants to say thanks for the *Personal Appointment Records,* and maybe because one or two of my letters caught his attention, he'll ask me to come in.

---

* *The Feldman Method,* Andrew H. Thomson, Farnsworth Publishing Co., Inc., Rockville Centre, N. Y.

15

MAKE THE CALLS AND THE SALES WILL FOLLOW

Ben, I'm sure that not everybody
agrees to see you when you walk in.
What do you do then?

You're right, maybe a man won't see me. Maybe his secretary will tell me he's too busy. And the chances are he *is* too busy. Every man has priorities, first things first— and does he know that I'm there to solve a problem for him? He doesn't. So why should I be first priority. Not yet, I'm not first priority. But I will be. I know I will be. So I say goodbye, and I plan to come back. And I *do* come back.

Or sometimes a man will come out to see you just to tell you that he can't see you. Why does he come out? Because he's a businessman—he's selling something, too, in his own way, no matter what his position in the company, and he wants people to be courteous to him when he sells so he's courteous to salesmen. Most men are courteous. When these men don't want to see you, they won't have their secretaries brush you off. They'll come out and meet you, maybe in the hallway. So say to this kind of man, "I just want to meet you. I have some ideas that may be of interest to you. I'd like to come back." What can he say—*don't* come back? Or you can say to him, "I represent New York Life. I've heard a lot about you. I'd like to say hello and show you some ideas that could help you with your business. I'd like to come back." Maybe that's as far as you'll get the first time. But you'll *come back*. You'll *come back*.

Don't take no for an answer. Keep coming back. Sooner or later if the man is in the right mood and he has a few minutes to spare, he'll say, "O.K., come on in. Glad to see you, but we'll have to make this fast." You have to work fast, make an impression fast. So say to this man, "May I show you something?" And this may be a probate record, showing how the day *before* some famous person died that person owed almost nothing, but the day *after* he died, that person's estate owed Uncle Sam hundreds of thousands or millions of dollars. This captures your prospect's attention, and you say to this man, "Look what happens to very successful people. You know what your problem is? You've been too successful. This could happen to you. Now, I have some ideas that may be of interest. I'd like to come back."

Come back. That's so important, so important. *Come back.* Have you heard the story of the agent who kept coming back, and coming back, and coming back? When they closed one door in his face, he came in another door?

And this kept on and on and on. So finally, the prospect—he was a good guy, he didn't want to be rude—finally, the prospect had to say, "Please. I appreciate your enthusiasm. But, please, don't come back for at least another five years." And the agent says, "O.K., I'll come back in five years. But if you're not here, who shall I ask for?"

That's what you have to do—just keep coming back.

How many calls on the average do you have to make before the call develops into an interview?

Sometimes, I have to make many, many calls.

But, you know, a call is a funny thing. Sometimes, when a man sees you, just a few words that you say can develop into an interview right there and then. That's why you must make the calls. There's no substitute for making calls. Make the calls and sales will follow.

Ben, I understand that you make as many as forty calls a month. You're very successful, and I know you have a big office. How do you manage it?

Yes, I have a busy office, a very busy office, and there are lots of things to be done, and they *are* done, but I still have time to go around and find prospects. You know why? I'll give you one reason:

I don't go flying all over the map. I don't travel except in my neck of the woods. My home is in East Liverpool, Ohio. I work within an area of forty to fifty miles from it. Traveling is wasting time. Because there are many, many, many people in my own back yard. I can call on them and still have time to do all the things that have to be done.

16

PROSPECTING: PEOPLE PLUS IDEAS

> *Do you always find a man's problem*
> *before you make a call?*

Not always.

> *Then what do you do?*

I go in to see that man—and I try to find out just what his problem is.

> *How do you do that?*

I prospect basically with ideas—ideas to merchandise cleancut, simple packages.

53

"Mr. Jones, I have money for sale. At a discount. You'll need that money some day to pay your taxes. May I present an idea that has been very valuable to a lot of people?"

Or:

"Mr. Smith, I have an idea which I think will be of interest. Are you interested in some tax-free money? You may need it some day to keep your company alive. I can help you develop that money. Will you listen?"

When prospecting, approach the man with a problem with disturbing questions. Keep asking disturbing questions and sooner or later you'll find the man's specific problem. When you talk to a man, you know what's important? Listening. Learn to listen. This is how you will find the problem.

Prospecting is basically recognizing the problem and making sure the problem has a price tag. And you know something?—when you find a prospect by pinpointing a man's problem, nine times out of ten, that prospect will become a policyholder.

17

THE BEST PROSPECT

How would you define the best prospect, Ben?

The best prospect is a man with a problem—all kinds of assets, but no money.

Where do you find the best prospects?

Among your clients. Why? Because your clients are prospects for *another* policy—for bigger coverage. Do you know that the biggest sales I made to close corporations—and I've worked with some 150 of them—were made to corporations where I had *already made sales.*

A lot of us write policies, then run away. Then somebody else comes along and writes another policy for the client we ran away from—and that new policy turns out to be *a bigger one than the policy we had placed.* So continue to prospect among your clients.

> *I'm sure that not all my clients*
> *are prospects for more insurance.*
> *How can I tell which of my clients*
> *are prospects?*

Watch them—and see which ones grow. The ones that grow—they're your prospects. You know, your people will grow—some of them, maybe all of them. And if you stay with them, *you'll* grow with them. I told you, my first sale was to a young businessman. A $2,000 policy. But he grew and I stayed with him, and, later on, he became the first man to buy a million dollar policy from me.

Why do I continue to sell to close corporations that I've already sold? Because they're *growing*—bringing in new key men—needing more working capital—getting bigger problems every day. I stay with them. When they have bigger problems, I call on them. My job—you know what it is? It's to solve those problems.

You know, cases will grow. There's no ceiling. Just stay with them, and you'll grow, too.

18

LOOKING DOWN THE ROAD

*I've heard that you can't always
wait until a client has grown to
sell him insurance. You look into
the man's future and find his
problems. Then you sell him today
the insurance he'll need tomorrow.
Is that right?*

Yes. I call that looking down the road. I say to a man:

"You need $100,000 to pay the taxes *today*—and here's a policy to cover it. But I know your company's making

money, I know you're in good health, so I have another policy
—and this is for *tomorrow*. *I'm looking down the road ten
years*. Then, you'll need $200,000 to pay your tax.

"And another thing: Your wife has a right to
income. So I have one designed for your salary continuation.
It pays her $30,000 a year for ten years. When you walk out,
your income goes on. Don't you want that for your wife?"

> *Ben, most of us base the amount*
> *of insurance a man should have*
> *on his current income. That's the*
> *accepted way. Do you think the*
> *accepted way of fixing the amount*
> *of life insurance a man should*
> *leave is wrong?*

I do. Another man's life isn't worth the same as
mine just because we have the same income *now*. Now—is that
forever? Doesn't a man *grow*? Some don't grow, of course.
But some *do*. Some of my clients have grown from local
businessmen to heads of national corporations. So what do I
try to do when I see them growing?—and you can see when
a company is growing, the signs are clear to read. What do
I do? I try to look down the road, see their problems which
don't yet exist, but will exist someday.

> *I can see that future problems*
> *can mean today's sales. But how*
> *can I convince a prospect to buy*
> *today for something he won't need*
> *until tomorrow?*

You're doing your client a great service when you
pinpoint the problems ahead of him and show him how *tomor-*

row his needs go up, but if he waits until tomorrow, *his rates go up*—and *his chance of getting life insurance goes down.* So, tell me, isn't it better for him to buy now?

If he can't afford whole life—and if he's growing, he may not be able to afford whole life—sell him term. You know what term is? It's an option on the future. He'll buy term *now*.

So—*sell ahead* and continue to look down the road among those clients you already *have* sold ahead to. One of my clients now has $5,000,000 worth of insurance with me. He's still growing, and I don't think he'll ever stop. I look down the road, and I'm sure he needs $5,000,000 *more*. What for? He has dreams, and he needs all that $10,000,000 to build a foundation under his dreams. I can help him make his dreams come true.

19

THE PHONE: SAY WHAT YOU HAVE TO SAY, THEN GET OFF

Ben, how do you set up the appointment for the interview once you've made a call and you're coming back? I know you often don't use the phone when you make your first calls, but don't you use the phone to set up an appointment when you're coming back, or when you want to see an old client?

Of course, I use the phone. But let me tell you something about telephones. Before you pick up the telephone, plan the words you're going to use. Know exactly what you're going to say. Say it. Then get off.

61

Sometimes, you know, I set up my first call by phone. This is my telephone approach:

"I represent New York Life. I've heard about you and would like to meet you. I specialize in discounting dollars. May I show you what I mean?"

Or suppose the man is a client and I know he's growing, and I know his problem will be growing in the future. I get on the phone and say:

"Mr. Jones, you know something?—you're a successful man. Most successful men are running so hard they never look far enough down the road. May I show you what I mean?"

Or, sometimes when I phone to set up an interview date after I've already made a call, I put the man's problem in the form of a question.

"Mr. Jones, how would you like to buy your partner's interest for pennies on the dollar? May I show you what I mean?"

"Sure, Ben, I'd like you to show me."

Then I say, "Would Tuesday at three or Friday at two be better?"

I give him a choice: one or the other. Not just one—not just, "How about Tuesday at three?" because he might say, "Sorry, Ben, I'm tied up then." But I give him a choice, and he's got to make a decision: one or the other.

"O.K., Ben, I'll look forward to seeing you Friday at two."

That's all you do on the phone. You can't sell successfully on the phone. Don't waste your ammunition.

20

HOW TO GET
A PROSPECT'S
ATTENTION

*Ben, I have this problem when I go
in on an interview: I talk to a man,
but he doesn't listen. His mind is
on other things. What should I do?*

You know, there are a hundred ways to close a
case, but there has to be a beginning. And the beginning is
getting the man's attention.

I walk in and I flip open my case, and the man
looks at what I've got in it, and says, "What's *that?*"

And I say, "It's what I sell. These come in packages of one hundred. How many packages would you like?" And you know what I sell? A thousand dollar bill! That gets the man's attention.

What does the man see? *A thousand dollar bill and three shiny new pennies.*

Now, why should I carry a thousand dollar bill? It's money. And money's funny—a man likes to look at money. And three pennies—that makes him wonder. "Why the three pennies, Ben? What do they mean?"

I tell him: "I'm selling dollars. For three pennies each."

Now he's going to *listen*. Money usually does this, especially when it appears that the money is pretty much something for nothing.

The money—it might look like it's something for nothing, but the man knows it can't be. "What's it all about, Ben?" He wants to know more.

When you get a man's attention, you know what you've done? You've done one of the most important things of all. It's the key. Why? The start of a sale is the interview. But the start of the interview is getting a man's attention. Unless you get his attention, you'll go no place.

21

THE KEY TO THE INTERVIEW IS THE DISTURBING QUESTION

Can you tell me what the purpose of the interview is as you see it, Ben?

The interview is to explore, to disturb, to pinpoint the problem, to move ahead by implied consent to the point when I say, "Let me put it together. You need a medical examination." I arrange it, and we go from there.

67

What would you say determines the
success of an interview?

The key to the sale is the interview, and the key to the interview is the disturbing question. I say to a man, "How much is time worth to you?" Or, "Could you give me one-third of everything you own *right now* without it hurting a little bit?" Or, "Would you like to insure one year's profits?"

In the interview, logic isn't enough. Use logic and emotion. Get the man stirred up. There's nothing like a disturbing question to build a fire under a man.

22

HOW TO CLOSE AN INTERVIEW: "LET ME PUT IT TOGETHER . . ."

You said that you end the interview
by saying "Let me put it together . . ."
That means you don't try for a sale
at the interview, do you?

That's correct. I say, "Let me put it together and you take a look."

"All right," the man will say, "you work it out and bring it back."

What's he got to lose? And even if he says nothing, he doesn't say "No." So you can still work it out and bring it back. In either case what you've done is lead the man to give you his *implied* consent.

How can a man say, "No"? You're not forcing the man to make a decision. You're not backing him into a sale. Never back a man into a corner and make him make a decision. Don't push. Lead.

23

GET HIM EXAMINED AND HE'S THREE-QUARTERS SOLD

What if the man says, "An examination!
Not again! I've just had one and my
doctor tells me I'm in wonderful shape."
What do I do, Ben?

You know what you ought to say to that man? "Yes, you're in wonderful shape now. But your doctor didn't

71

tell you how you'll be *ten years from now*. You see, we're going to take a look at how long you're going to live. Don't you want to know?"

He wants to know.

Say to him, "Suppose I set it up?"

What if the man says, "Oh, I can't
spare the time for a medical exam"?
What do I say?

Say to this man, "You know, we may be pinpointing your problem, but we may find there's very little we can do about it. Medically, I mean. Let's find out."

And you know something?—now that he's implied that he wants insurance, it worries him that he may not be able to get it. If you see him hesitating, disturb him more. Say: "I'm not sure at this point if all this talk about solving your problem is not a little premature. You know, there's a price tag on success. You know what that price tag is? A man gradually begins to fall apart. His pressure goes up. This goes wrong, that goes wrong. And, you know, you wait too long. The medical committee—well, the price you pay for success is certainly not going to help you with them. But, anyway, let's see. Let's see how much our life underwriting committee feels your life is worth."

I sometimes get a man who says,
"There's nothing wrong with me."
How do I get him to get an exam?

Say to this man: "Let me make sure you're as good on the inside as you look on the outside. Could be you've waited too long. As the years go by, a man pays a price for success. Mother nature makes us a little bit older. And older doesn't mean better. Let's see if you can qualify."

Now, just because he thinks he may not be able to get it, he wants it. Now he *wants* to qualify. He'll *take* the exam.

*Just how successful are you, Ben, in
getting a man to take an examination?*

When I say to a man, "Let's find out if I can get this for you. All I need now is underwriting, which means a medical examination. Suppose I set it up. Then I'll put it together, and you can take a look at what I have." Nine times out of ten, he'll go along. I haven't forced him into a decision. I won't let him make a decision. I'll wait for the medical O.K. No sense selling the policy until I can get it. Don't sell the policy first. *Get* it first.

24

THE SALE:
GETTING READY
TO GET READY

Suppose I get a medical o.k.
How do I present the policy?

Thoroughly understand the policy that you're going to propose and why you picked the policy, and why you picked the amount. Thoroughly understand the plan and what it will do for the applicant. Let there be no doubt in your mind that you understand why he needs the policy and why he needs that much coverage. Let me say to you that the more you know about the applicant and his family, and what he wants done, and why he wants it done, the better able you are to fit the policy to the man. I've told you already, selling

insurance is like a tailor with a bolt of cloth. It'll be up to
you to make it fit.

How do I make a policy fit a man?

Is one man like another? Are one man's problems
like another man's problems? Every man is different. Every
man's problems are different. When you begin to work out the
details, you see the differences. Two estate packages—they're
different. The details are different. You've got to work out
these details. That's the way you fit a policy to a man. I spend
more time creating the case in my mind than I do selling it.
I work it over and over again. Just when I get to the point
where I *believe* it—where I'm sure it's right for the man—
suddenly, I'm not so sure—suddenly, I want to make a change.
And I do just that. I change it. So my girls—they think I'm
crazy. But I must know I'm right, and that the policy is right
for the man. I call all this getting ready to get ready.

*How much time should I spend
getting ready to get ready?*

Be careful about overdoing things—taking too much
time. So many men spend so much time getting ready that
they never get ready. Take just enough time to get the job
done right. When a job is right, you know it—because you
believe it. Any more time than enough time is wasted time.

25

THE ILLUSTRATION: HOW TO MERCHANDISE IT

When I come back to the prospect, I have something with me which I've made up—something in the way of an *illustration*. My illustration is open face. It looks simple. It *is* simple. But, remember, a lot of work went into making it simple. You just don't throw an illustration together.

ONE
HUNDRED
THOUSAND
DOLLAR POLICY

BONUS POLICY

JOHN DOE

End Of Year	Annual Premium	Increase In Cash Value	THIS IS YOUR NET COST	Face Value +	Accumulated Cash Value +	Dividend Account* =	Total Death Benefit
1)	—	—	[$2,383]		—	—	$100,000
2)		$ 1,800	[583]		$ 1,800	$ 151	101,951
3)		2,000	[383]		3,800	456	104,256
4)		2,100	[283]		5,900	906	106,806
5)	$ 2,383	2,100	[283]	$100,000	8,000	1,523	109,523
6)		2,200	[183]		10,200	2,273	112,473
7)		2,200	[183]	TAX-FREE	12,400	3,156	115,556
8)		2,200	[183]		14,600	4,158	118,758
9)		2,300	[83]		16,900	5,268	122,168
10)		2,400	[- 17]		19,300	6,480	125,780
TOTAL	$23,830	$19,300	[$4,530]				
AVERAGE	$ 2,383	$ 1,930	[$ 453]				

THIS IS YOUR INSURANCE RETURN

*Dividend account is paid-up additions and figures shown represent face amount of paid-up insurance.
Dividends are based on current illustrations and are not guarantees of future dividend results.

78

*Ben, I can see that you've worked
out the solution to the man's specific
problem in detail. I'm sure you've
worked hard to get the right facts and
the right figures. What impresses me
is that all those facts and figures—
well, they don't look dull. They look
exciting. How do you do it?*

I use good paper. I use good typing equipment. I use color. I give the illustration a name. And I put the man's name on the illustration. An illustration might read: A BONUS POLICY FOR JOHN JONES. Notice the dollar bill. Why is it there? Because my illustrations are bundles of money. I'm selling money.

Learn to merchandise. But don't get carried away; don't let *how* you present the picture complicate the picture. Your illustration must be simple, because unless it *is* simple, your prospect won't understand it. And if he doesn't understand it—know what happens? He won't buy it.

26

NEVER UNDERESTIMATE A MAN'S NEEDS

*On that illustration you just showed me,
Ben—those figures! That's a lot of
money. Don't you find those major amounts
hard to sell?*

His problem has a price tag. The price tag has to be paid. Either his family pays it with dollars or he pays it with pennies. Which is better? Aren't you helping him? The bigger the price tag, the more you're helping him. He *needs* that policy. Never underestimate his needs. When you underestimate his needs, you're *not* helping him. When you think small, you're actually hurting the man you should be helping.

Tell him what he needs—no matter how big it looks. Then you're truly helping him.

When I come back, the prospect really doesn't know how much I'm going to bring him. Maybe in his mind, he has a picture of $100,000 *now,* but in a year from now—what will he need? A half a million. So I come back with a policy for a half a million. He doesn't buy the half a million—that's too much for him because he can't see down the road that far. But you know what happens? He doesn't want the hundred thousand, and he doesn't buy the half a million, but he does take something inbetween. You don't wind up with the $100,000, you don't wind up with the half a million—you wind up with, say, $350,000.

> *That's a lot of money, Ben. Those are awfully big figures you throw around. I get tongue-tied when I have to say to a man, "Buy something worth . . ." You see, I stutter. I just can't get myself to say, "A half million dollars." Can you give me some advice?*

Have you ever thought how funny it is that a man will insure everything he owns for what it's worth—*except* his life? He has a car he has insured. For how much? For pretty much what it's worth. He has a home he has insured. For how much? For pretty much what it's worth. The one thing he doesn't insure for what it's worth is his life. Apparently, it isn't worth much.

He'll insure his life for only five or ten percent of what it's worth. The most precious thing in the world, insured for only five to ten percent of its value! Isn't that a little crazy?

The home is replaceable, the car is replaceable—but a man's life . . .? In enough time a man can buy a new car or build a new home—but, tell me, with all the time in the world, how can he get a new life?

The *value* of a man's life—why should you stop thinking big when you think of a man's life? What's bigger? Do you know of anything that's bigger? Tell me something: How much is *your* life worth? Want to know how much? How much did you insure it for? Well, *that's* what it's worth—no more, no less. Is your life worth as little as the value you put on it? Can you ever put *too much* value on your life? There are people who are insured for fifty thousand dollars; there are people who are insured for five hundred thousand dollars; there are people who are insured for millions of dollars—but *there is no one insured for more than his life is worth.*

There's no one who will be willing to trade all his tomorrows for his life insurance; there's not a man in the world who'd be willing to do that. Don't be afraid to put a big price tag on a man's life.

You know, you become the most important person in the world when, at the end of a year, you've sold a million dollars worth of insurance. Why? Because as sure as you're sitting there, one million dollars walks in because of what you did. And that one million dollars walks in when a widow needs it most, when a company needs it most, when a family needs it most.

> *Ben, I have my own kind of*
> *"money fright." I mean it's my*
> prospect *who has all that money, not me.*
> *That makes it hard for me to sell.*
> *What shall I do?*

I never had any money as a young man. I was a poor boy. You know what I earned on my first job? Ten dollars a week. I admit the other man's money scared me.

But when I went in to see a man, and he had money, and I didn't have so much money, I said to myself, "You know, tax is a great leveler of income, and just because he's made ten thousand—or a hundred times ten thousand—that doesn't mean that he's got that money. The man who makes a little more, spends a little more. The man who makes a little more, pays a little more tax. The man who makes a little more, gives a little more to charity, and so on and so on."

May I ask you: How many men with million dollar estates die with only a few thousand dollars in cash in the bank? Money's funny: sometimes the more you have, the less you have. So when you think of it *that* way, you can walk in feeling that that man's money is nothing to be scared of.

27

WHAT TO ANSWER WHEN THE PROSPECT SAYS, "I'VE GOT TO TAKE IT UP WITH..."

Ben, when you get to the stage of showing figures—and particularly big figures— doesn't the man almost always say, "I've got to take it up with my accountant or my attorney?" What do you do then?

That's an objection you frequently meet. It can hurt. It can hurt the man and it can hurt you. That's because accountants and attorneys tend to delay. They raise objections which put doubts in a man's mind. These people could stop a sale. Let me go over how I handle this type of objection, because it's important, very important.

Let's take the accountant. An accountant is a very important person. Tell me, could a businessman get along without an accountant? The accountant figures out the truth in figures, and he's needed. He says two and two make four; and if you go to the bank and borrow ten thousand dollars, he'll put the ten thousand dollars on the balance sheet, and he'll tell you that you have a liability of ten thousand dollars. But will he *pay* the ten thousand dollars? Will he pay *any* of the bills? No, he won't. He'll just figure them up.

But some day there's going to be debts to pay—to Uncle Sam, or to the bank. He'll figure out the bills that have to be paid, all right. But when the chips are down, *he* won't pay them. He'll figure out the amount of cash owed. But he can't *create* the cash. Someone has to pay those bills. Know what I tell the prospect? I tell him all I've just told you about his accountant, I add:

"The tax must be paid—unless Uncle Sam will treat you differently than anybody else. Who's going to pay the tax—the accountant? Somebody has to pay the tax. And the day it becomes payable, that'll be the day I walk in with enough money to pay it. I promise you it *will* get paid! Can your accountant make that promise?"

Take the lawyer. He's important, too. The businessman needs him. He does a good job, a necessary job. But be careful. The lawyer can take the case away from you. A lawyer can stop a case from moving—and once a case stops moving, the case is dead. What good is a lawyer unless he finds something wrong? Do you think he's going to say, "That's a wonderful thing, Feldman!"

When a man says to you, "I have to show this to my lawyer," say to that man:

"Fine! But what is it that you're going to show to your lawyer? The only thing I want to do is *create* money. Can your lawyer do that? Is he an expert in *creating* money? Your lawyer is a wonderful person. You need him. But he doesn't pay the bills. I think we should all stay in our back yards. The lawyer's job—that's to *distribute* money. My job is to do what no one else can do. To *create* money. If I don't create it, he'll have nothing to distribute."

The basic purpose of the life insurance salesman is to create, and not get all wrapped up in something that's the job of the lawyer, the accountant or the banker, or someone else. Our job is to create cash, not to distribute it. Make that clear to a man.

28

THE PREMIUM: NEVER LOOK FOR EXTRA MONEY

*Let's get back to big packages.
They mean big premiums. Suppose I make
my presentation and the man says, "I
buy everything you say—but I just
don't have the money to buy the policy."
Where do I look for that man's extra
money so he can pay the premiums?*

There is no such thing as extra money. None of us
has extra money. We make a little more, so we live a little
better. We make a little more, so we buy a second car. We
make a little more, because we like to have some of the better

things of life; we'd like to have a home on the lake, why not? So between buying more and Uncle Sam saying, "Whoa, whoa, I'm your partner. You make a little more, so I want a little more," you'll find most men never having any *extra* money. And no matter what it is you're selling, *if you look for extra money, you won't find it. Never look for extra money. There isn't any.*

The mistake a lot of us make, you see, is to look for *extra* money. If you reach down in a man's pocket for his wallet, he'll break your arm.

29

FINDING THE PREMIUM MONEY: A MAN'S FAMILY COMES FIRST

If there's no extra money, Ben, how's the man able to pay the premiums?

All men, when the chips are down, will put their families first. That's top priority. When I was selling smaller policies, I would say to a man:

"You need a system of priorities. First things should come first. Do you want your family to go on living the way you've accustomed them to living? Well, let's look at the picture. They need $10,000 a year to live. Maybe when you're gone, they can get by with $8,000, or $7,000 or some lesser amount. And how much insurance did you say you had? Thirty thousand? Fine, they can live on that for three years, four years, five years at the most. Now, how old is your little boy? Six years old? Let's say the money will last for five years, how old will he be then? Eleven? Eleven—is that old enough for him to stand on his own feet?—old enough for him to start earning enough to see himself through school and college?"

This could tear a man apart. What I was saying to him was real, very real. I'd say to that man: "Thirty thousand dollars. That's fine. But divide that by time—the time that's necessary to do the things your widow will have to do: pay off the home, educate the children, meet the medical expenses —time to do a lot of things, make many dreams come true. How much time will $30,000 underwrite?"

He understood he needed more insurance—but he didn't have the extra money for the premiums. What did he do? He took a little bit from here, a little bit from there. He didn't have any *extra* money, but he *had* money, and he diverted enough of it from other things to pay the premiums. Why? Because he'd established priorities: his family came first.

But, Ben, those were small policies— small premiums. It wasn't too hard to find the money. But didn't you find it harder to find the money when you began to sell bigger policies?

I would say to a man: "When you save money in a bank, that's an accumulation. But we create money for you.

Who else can do that? You may need the money we create. How do you know you have enough time? If you do have enough time, we'll give you your money back. But if you don't have enough time, the money we create will keep your widow going. You might not make quite as much money with us as if you invested your money in a bank, but you know what *we're* going to do? *We're going to make darned sure that your family has a right to go on living.*

"You know, I have a $100,000 insurance for *my* family. You've only got $50,000—and yet you earn as much money as I do, maybe more. You live in a house just as nice as mine. You want the same things for your children as I want for mine. You know what I want for them?

"I want the right to send them to school. An education costs money. Do you think you'll have enough money? If you begin paying for that education now, when your little boy is five years old, you'll have 13 years to pay for it. But if you wait until he's ready for college, will *you* be ready? If you can't pay for it slowly over a period of years, why do you think you'll be able to pay for it all at once? And you know, the odds will be that when your neighbor's little boy goes to college—*yours won't.*"

That shook the man up. That made the man know that to find that money for premiums was his first priority. Believe me, he found that money.

So what you do when you talk to a man is show him that need to put first things first—to put his family first. Say to a man:

"Your family has a right to go on living. And living the way you want them to go on living, that costs money. Somebody's got to pay that cost whether you buy the policy or not. There is a cost either way: if you do or if you don't. If you do you can pay for it with three cent dollars. If you don't, your family can pay for it by doing without. Doing without *what?* Doing without living in a nice home. Doing without an education for the children. Doing without having the nice things you're so happy to give them."

You hit a man hard, you build a fire under him. So he looks for the money to pay the premiums. He'll take the money from his savings, his investments, maybe he won't smoke so many expensive cigars. He'll spend a little less, but you know what? He'll come up with the premiums.

Ben, what about when you get into the field of large estates, close corporations, partnerships—when there's really big money involved—what do you say to a man who says to you, "Sure, Ben, I know I need the policy, but where's the money to come from?"

I say to this man:

"You know, the money has to come from someplace. This policy can't be free. If it were, it wouldn't be much good. But so far as paying the premiums: there's a price tag on doing it; there's a price tag on *not* doing it. Doing nothing doesn't solve your problem; it only postpones it. You have a right to postpone it. But if you postpone solving your problem, you know who'll have to solve it? Your wife. Only she won't be your wife. She'll be your widow. And your whole family, your son and daughter as well as your wife— because she's going to need help—together, they'll have to do with hundred-cent dollars what you *should* have done with *discounted dollars.* If you have trouble paying pennies on the dollar, do you think your family will have it easy paying what must be paid with full hundred-cent dollars?"

So the appeal is once again: A man's family comes first. Is that right, Ben?

A man doesn't want to see everything he's worked all his life for go down the drain. He doesn't want to see Uncle Sam and other creditors take everything. He doesn't want the creditors to come first. He wants his family to come first. I say to this man:

"I know there isn't any extra money. If you make a lot, you pay out a lot. You spend more, you pay more taxes. I'm in the same boat. But it's a question of some things come first and some things come second. Your creditors should not come first. Your family should not come second. You've spent thirty years putting your estate together. For whom? Your creditors? Or for your family? Do you want to keep what you worked for? Do you want your family to have what is rightfully theirs—everything you worked for?"

Ben, you know I tried this approach, and my prospect said to me, "I agree with everything you said, but can you tell me where I can squeeze say four thousand dollars or five thousand dollars out of my till? That money is after taxes—and that's an important consideration. Tell me: Where's the money going to come from to do exactly what you think I should do?" How would I answer that man, Ben?

I would say:

"I know there's a big flow of money through your corporation—that's where the money's going to come from. But if three hundred dollars a month makes that much difference, you're already broke and you don't know it."

That stirs a man up.

30

TAKE THE PREMIUMS FROM CAPITAL, AND TAKE IT AWAY FROM THE TAX COLLECTOR

You just told me how a man can find the premiums in the cash flow of his corporation. Is there any other way you can help a man find the premiums so they don't have to come out of his current income?

For older people in particular, tell them:

"Don't take the premiums from income, take them from capital. Why? Because when you do that, you take it away from the tax collector."

97

I have a gentleman in mind who's paying $30,000 a year in premiums—and that's a pretty good chunk of money. You know, this man could pay that money out of income, but why should he? He'd still have to pay income taxes on it.

I have lots of clients who take their premiums out of capital.

31

DIVIDENDS: USE THEM TO EXPAND COVERAGE

Is there any other specific source of money for premiums?

When I prospect, I check through our Central Service Office to see if a man has a policy. Sometimes he has. Sometimes the *dividends have mounted up. There's* the money! I say to this man:

"Look, we already have the money. If you leave it the way it is, you have $15,000 piled up in dividends. But put that $15,000 to work with me, and if something happens, we'll pay the claim *and* give you back the $15,000."

Once they buy a policy, most men pay little attention to it. They pay attention to paying the premiums, yes. But they usually pay no attention to dividends. Once a year, when the premium comes due, they pay it—and that's it. And then they forget about the policy for another year. Dividends quite often are left to accumulate. *And it's from dividends that I find that I can begin new policies.* So I tell a man:

"We've already got your money. All we have to do is make sure that you're still eligible for it. Suppose I put it together and you take a look. All we need is medical underwriting. I'll set up an exam, and we'll go from there."

I had a case where a man had built up substantial coverage over the years, and had accumulated a large number of dollars in dividends. One day I said to this man:

"Lou, you know something?—your program is a bit out of balance. We've done a good job in regard to *your* part of the program. But you know, you have a marital deduction, which means that one-half of your estate will be tax-free only because it goes to your wife. But what happens then? While the money isn't taxable in *your* estate, it will be taxable in *her* estate. So why don't we create a little better balance in your overall program. *Why not use some of the dividends that have accumulated—that are continuing to be earned on your overall program to set up a policy for her?*"

He liked the idea. I had her examined. The policy was issued. It was the simplest sale in the world. Know why? *I already had the money for the premiums.*

I had another case along these lines. I had the man examined, and there had been some changes, and we turned him down. Meanwhile, a lot of dividends had piled up. He had almost $30,000 in dividend accumulations, and between $6,000 and $8,000 in annual dividends coming in each year. I couldn't insure this man. But you know what I did? I insured his son. Instead of writing the father $200,000, I wrote the son $500,000! *The dividends on the father's insurance—* dividends that had accumulated—dividends that will be earned each year—*those dividends pay the premiums on the son's insurance.* Simplest sale in the world!

There are dozens of sales like these that you can pick up. Say to a man:

"I can expand your coverage by twenty-five percent and you don't have to take a cent out of your pocket. I already have the money. Let me put it together and you take a look."

PART 2

32

HOW TO CREATE PACKAGES WITH BIG PRICE TAGS

You call yourself a "package salesman."
Ben, can you give me some guidelines on how
I can create packages with big price tags?

The packages you create are *real*. They're made to fit *real* problems. They're made to solve problems. *Serious* problems. Serious—why? Because either the man has to pay or his family has to pay.

When you're creating a package, your imagination has to be in high gear. You work *first* with your *imagination*— it's got to be in your *mind* first—then you work with words and facts and figures.

I'm a young man just starting.
Can I go after the larger policies?

You see where you're going to stub your toe: you're not quite ready to talk about the big policy from the standpoint of tax impact on the estate, of dollars to pay what must be paid. Are you familiar with what takes place when a man walks out—the tax impact? Have you studied the estate table to know how much it will be?

As a young man, you must pay the price in study, you must be able to take the problem apart to understand what makes and creates a problem today and tomorrow. It isn't that difficult to do. It takes time—but what doesn't take time? If you're willing to do that, then you can do so much good for so many people.

What are the areas I must study up on
to sell larger policies?

Most of my problems arise from close corporations, partnerships, and family-held companies. I build my packages around a few fundamental problems, because these problems have big price tags. These problems concern: Estate taxes, company continuity, income taxes, guaranteed markets, key men, corporate credit, and similar areas. Later on, I'll answer your questions about them in some detail.

How long would it take me to learn how to
sell a larger package?

If you worked at it, spending some time every day on basic background as it involves tax structure and the life insurance contract, I would say within a year you would have acquired a basic background that would permit you to go out and do this kind of work.

Are there any courses I should take?

I don't know where you could go other than to your own company for the sort of information you're looking for. When you get into a case, go to your manager and tell him what you have in mind. Let him go to the advanced underwriting department in your home office to help you put the case together. They're familiar with cases involving major amounts. They know how to do it.

There are agents in your company who are doing it. Go with an agent like that on a case or two. On your first case or so, why **not give** that agent the commission, and he'll give you the know-how and the procedure? Then do it yourself.

Work at it, and it will work. Instead of writing 50 cases at $10,000 apiece—that's a half-million dollars—write one case at a million dollars.

You know something, the big man with the big problem is easier to sell than the small man with the small problem. Because the big man is accustomed to using banks and corporate credit-lines; he's not taking the money out of his own pocket. He's using the corporate pocketbook. He doesn't hesitate to have the corporation buy something if it's the right thing to do. The bank won't object to putting up the money either, because that money is going to keep the company strong.

Prove to yourself what I'm telling you. Jump in. Get your feet wet. You may stub your toe a time or two in the beginning, but you'll become stronger for it. It *will* work. Your cases *will* get bigger and bigger and bigger. They'll get *even* bigger if you remember to *look down the road*. The man grows, the company grows, the problem grows.

That's how you create bigger cases with major amounts. I like this sort of work. To me, it's not real work. I start and I don't stop!

Ben, can you give me a very brief example
of how you create a case?

I spend hour after hour creating a case, making it logical, then making it simple. For example, I know a man with an estate worth roughly $8,000,000. When that man goes, the estate tax will take about half of that $8,000,000. It's very difficult to pull $4,000,000 out of $8,000,000 without wrecking that man's company. It leaves a big hole. I say to this man:

"Do it my way. The premium on a $4,000,000 policy is about $25,000 a month. The interest on a $4,000,000 loan is also about $25,000 a month. If you pay the interest, we'll pay the principal. If you don't do it my way, you'll have to do it your way."

Make it logical. Then make it simple. When you do, you'll sell it.

33

STUDY ESTATES: THE PRICE TAGS REACH SEVEN FIGURES

What made you turn to the problems of estates to write policies involving major amounts?

I began to study estates. Study them and you'll find that in estates of a hundred thousand dollars, of a million dollars, of ten million dollars, there was almost no money— no cash. The men who had accumulated these estates had all kinds of other assets, such as stock, buildings, machinery, land, but they didn't have much cash. And it's only money that Uncle Sam wants when these men die.

The day a man walks out, Uncle Sam walks in and asks for one-third of everything that man owned. Could you, right now, pay out one-third of everything you own? It's simply not feasible to carry the amount of cash required to pay inheritance taxes. But the day you walk out, the government walks in, and they want cash. Furthermore, they have a way of getting it.

Where's the cash to come from? *From* the estate? That's *forced* liquidation. Liquidation of assets while a man is here is one thing, but after he's gone, it may be entirely different. It may not be an *"orderly"* liquidation. When a buyer knows the widow has to sell—isn't the buyer going to offer a low price? Somebody may get the estate for one-half of what it's worth. A man must either create cash to absorb the tax impact, or the tax impact will absorb the estate.

The function of life insurance is to create cash. I say to a man:

"It's better to use insurance to pay your estate taxes. While you'll pay $500,000 for your tax, you'll pay very little for the $500,000. And your estate remains intact."

34

HOW TO CONDUCT AN ESTATE INTERVIEW

Ben, I wonder if you can give me the highlights of an estate interview?

I might open by saying to a man:

"Very nice of you to see me. You know, Mr. Jones, you've been running pretty hard now for about 30 years and in spite of the tax structure you've built a beautiful estate. Now I presume you built this estate for your family. May I show you what happens in most estates?"

Here's what I show him:

WILLIAM WOODWARD, JR.
Prominent Sportsman and Financier
Oyster Bay, New York

Died October 30, 1955, at age 35

Gross Estate $11,063,946
Total Costs 7,443,494

Net Estate ... . $ 3,620,452

Cash in Estate, $553,041

SETTLEMENT COSTS

Debts .... $ 543,869
Admn. Expense 241,628
Attorney's Fee 350,000
Executor's Fee 439,211
N.Y. Estate Tax 1,206,725
*Federal Estate Tax 4,662,061
  TOTAL COSTS $7,443,494

Debts Day
Before Death

DEFICIT $6.890.000

*No marital deduction.

OVER 67% SHRINKAGE

DWIGHT D. EISENHOWER
34th U.S. President
Gettysburg, Pennsylvania

Died March 28, 1969, at age 78

Gross Estate $2,905,857

Total Costs 671,429
_____
Net Estate $2,234,428

Cash in Estate, $60,820

* Full marital deduction. Widow has life estate from Trust Funds. These figures are only first and partial accounting filed to date.

(1) Includes over $6,500 to run farm until crops harvested and sold.

OVER 23% SHRINKAGE

© Estate Research Company 1973, P. O. Box 2157, Castro Valley, California 94546

SETTLEMENT COSTS

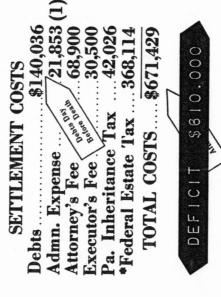

Debts	$140,036
Admn. Expense	21,853 (1)
Attorney's Fee	68,900
Executor's Fee	30,500
Pa. Inheritance Tax	42,026
*Federal Estate Tax	368,114
TOTAL COSTS	$671,429

DEFICIT $610,000

*Full marital deduction.

113

JOHN F. JELKE

Chairman, John F. Jelke Co., Oleomargarine Manufacturers

Chicago, Illinois

Died January 1, 1965, at age 77

Gross Estate	$6,971,664
Total Costs	3,778,519
Net Estate	$3,193,145

Cash in Estate, $227,856

Included in the gross estate is $115,000 of life insurance.

OVER 54% SHRINKAGE

SETTLEMENT COSTS

Debts	$ 4,902
Admn. Expense	179,376
Attorney's Fee	140,000
Executor's Fee	140,000
Ill. Inheritance Tax	549,870
*Federal Estate Tax	2,764,371
TOTAL COSTS	$3,778,519

Debt's Day
Before Death

DEFICIT $3,551,000

*No marital deduction; no spouse surviving.

© 1973 Estate Research Company, P.O. Box 2157, Castro Valley, California 94546

114

HUMPHREY BOGART
PROMINENT ACTOR

Humphrey Bogart was born in New York City, the son of Dr. Belmont de Forest and Maud (Humphrey) Bogart. According to **Who's Who in the Theatre** he was born on January 23, 1899; according to the Warner Brothers Publicity Department he was born on December 25, 1900 ("but demands birthday presents as well as Christmas presents"). His father was a prominent New York surgeon and his mother was interested in art.

Bogart got his first acting part in 1920 with a road company and he made his first appearance on a New York stage in 1922. For the next thirteen years Bogart played roles of various dimensions in a long succession of plays. Some were successes, some did moderately well, others were out and out failures; but Bogart was rarely unemployed. Bogart took a number of screen tests before he landed a motion picture role and was actually in motion pictures commencing in 1930.

Motion picture critics, as well as the less critical motion picture going public, found Bogart an exceptionally competent actor. He told reporters that "all I do to look evil is to let my beard grow for two days", but critics thought he was merely being modest. He could drop his accurate English and fall into the clipped jargon of the underworld; he could snarl or cringe, be suave or crudely sinister, and all apparently without effort.

DIED JANUARY 14, 1957, AGE 57

Gross Estate	$910,146.
Total Settlement Costs	**274,234.**
Net Estate	$635,912.

EXCERPTS FROM
THE LAST WILL AND TESTAMENT
OF
HUMPHREY BOGART

Humphrey Bogart died on January 14, 1957. He was fifty-seven years old. With one-half of his estate, the actor set up a trust for his wife, directing that the distribution of any part of that trust to the widow was to be determined solely by the executors other than herself. In explanation of the arrangement, Bogart stated in his will that "I am particularly aware of her [actress Lauren Bacall] high earning potential, the impact of income taxes thereon, the standard of living to which she has been accustomed during our marriage, and the uncertainties of the many years during which I hope her life will continue in the event of my decease."

After the encroachment of death taxes, the remainder of the actor's estate was used to create trusts benefiting the couple's two children. Upon reaching the age of twenty-three, the son and daughter were to receive the full income of the trust, as well as $25,000 in cash. Instructions for further distribution directed that no less than half the balance of the trust was to go to the son by age thirty-five, and all by forty, while the daughter was to have obtained at least half of her trust by her forty-fifth birthday.

Final instructions of the will directed that, in the event that trust funds cannot be disposed of due to failure of issue, the trustees were to establish the Humphrey Bogart Foundation with the remaining corpus. The foundation would serve primarily to benefit medical research, with an emphasis on cancer.

Those named executors and trustees were the testator's widow, a friend and the Security-First National Bank of Los Angeles.

The Settlement Costs:

Debts	$101,767
Administration Expense	3,988
Attorney's Fee	11,249
Executor's Fee	11,249
California Inheritance Tax	21,325
Federal Estate Tax*	124,655
TOTAL SETTLEMENT COSTS	$274,234

*50% Marital Deduction

Cash in estate $25,693

Now what are they? They are actual probate records. They're published by a little company, known as "Your Estate." They cost next to nothing. I think for $10.00 a year, you get these records every 90 days.

Now what do I do with the probate records as they come to me? I pick out those that I think will have impact—names people will recognize—and I blow up the records to several times the size I get them.

I put these blow-ups in front of a man, and I say to him:

"May I show you what happens to millionaires? You may recognize names because these cases are authentic. Look what happened in this case. The executor went out and borrowed $150,000 to prevent a forced liquidation.

"Look at another one here. Do you remember Humphrey Bogart the actor? Look what happened. He had everything—except money. Now, he didn't owe a lot of money. Lots of men die owing almost nothing, but the next day they owe hundreds of thousands of dollars—maybe, millions of dollars. They call it taxes.

"Here is Gordon Stouffer of Cleveland, Ohio. He had a $2-million estate. How much did he owe the day before he died? Less than $50,000. How much cash did he have? Not much. Maybe $17,000. But the day after he died, he owed $550,000! And he still only had $17,000 in cash. How did the estate get the cash it needed to pay the government? They have a name for this. You know what they call it? Liquidation."

GORDON A. STOUFFER
Chairman, Stouffer Corp., Restaurant Chain, Cleveland, Ohio

Died June 6, 1958, age 51

Gross Estate............$1,937.477.

Total Costs.............. 552,071.

Net Estate...............$1,385,406.
Cash in estate, $17,771.

SETTLEMENT COSTS
Debts...........................$197,446.
Administration Expense...   8,503.
Attorney's Fee ....   50,000.
Executor's Fee...............   38,820.
Ohio Inheritance Tax ....   32,653.
*Federal Estate Tax......... 224,649.
   TOTAL COSTS............$552,071.
*50% marital deduction

© ESTATE RESEARCH CO.

The man I'm talking to has done like most other men; that is, made a lot of money, locked it in one thing or another. He has no ready cash right now to pay the government. You show him what happened to so and so, and to so and so, and you build a fire beneath him.

*How do you show the man
the effect of the tax impact
on his own estate?*

I present an Estate Tax Table in color that shows him how much of what he owns isn't his, and a discounted dollar illustration showing mathematically that he can buy dollars for pennies apiece.

JOHN DOE

ONE HUNDRED THOUSAND DOLLAR POLICY

THIS IS YOUR INSURANCE RETURN

End Of Year	Annual Premium	Increase In Cash Value	THIS IS YOUR NET COST	Face Value +	Accumulated Cash Value +	Dividend Account* =	Total Death Benefit
1)		—	[$2,383]		—	—	$100,000
2)		$ 1,800	[583]		$ 1,800	$ 151	101,951
3)		2,000	[383]		3,800	456	104,256
4)		2,100	[283]		5,900	906	106,806
5)	$ 2,383	2,100	[283]	$100,000	8,000	1,523	109,523
6)		2,200	[183]		10,200	2,273	112,473
7)		2,200	[183]	TAX-FREE	12,400	3,156	115,556
8)		2,200	[183]		14,600	4,158	118,758
9)		2,300	[83]		16,900	5,268	122,168
10)		2,400	[- 17]		19,300	6,480	125,780
TOTAL	$23,830	$19,300	[$4,530]				
AVERAGE	$ 2,383	$ 1,930	[$ 453]				

GROSS COST PER DOLLAR — 19 CENTS

NET COST PER DOLLAR — 4 CENTS

*Dividend account is paid-up additions and figures shown represent face amount of paid-up insurance. Dividends are based on current illustrations and are not guarantees of future dividend results.

118

I say to a man:

"Let me show you the part of your estate that isn't yours." And that part could be in six figures or in seven figures. "Could you write me a check for that amount without it hurting a little bit? I'm not saying it'll break your company, but wouldn't it bend it?

"So why do you want to run hard for 30 years and then have 15 years go down the drain? You know there's a price if you do something or you don't do something. Most estates, some day, fall apart—not because you did something wrong, but because you did nothing; that's what's wrong."

I can see the logic of your approach. The man wants to know what he can do to keep his estate from falling apart, and you tell him how he can do it with discounted dollars. **Is that right?**

Yes, he doesn't want to see his estate fall apart. I show him that it *will* fall apart if he doesn't take action *now*, because if he waits too long—the man is getting on in years—he won't be able to get insurance. I say to this man:

"Mr. Jones, the taxes must be paid *from* your estate —or *for* your estate. Let me pay it *for* your estate—with discounted dollars. Pulling the amount of cash the tax collector wants out of the estate leaves a hole *in* the estate—quite often a big hole—something *so* big a lot of things fall apart. It's better to use insurance to pay the tax collector than take it out of the estate. While you pay two hundred thousand dollars for the tax, you'll pay very little for the two hundred thousand dollars.

"So put me on the payroll. I'll work for five hundred dollars a month. The day you walk out, two hundred thousand dollars walks in. And while you're paying in premiums, you're piling up cash. When you need it, you can get it."

Yes, I say, "Put me on your payroll." Just exactly that. Other companies are accustomed to putting people on the payroll. One person more or less doesn't make much difference. You know, you could be the most important person on his payroll—because the day he walks out, you walk in with enough cash to pay everything that must be paid.

How do you close, Ben?

I might say to the man:

"Mr. Jones, part of what you own isn't yours. It belongs to the tax collector. And yet if an estate is worth building, it's worth keeping. Even though you paid income tax all your life, part of what you have left still isn't yours. And the day you walk out, Uncle Sam walks in and he'll want a great big chunk of your estate. Furthermore, he has a way of getting it. You have a problem; if you don't do something about it, if you don't solve it, you simply postpone it; some day, someone will have to do something about it. If you can qualify, I've got discounted dollars—dollars for pennies apiece. My dollars cost roughly 3¢ per dollar per year. It'll take a long time to pay in the amount we guarantee to pay out. I'm sure you don't want the tax load falling on your family. Let's use my plan. Suppose I put it together and you take a look."

35

A SPECIAL SALES AID FOR THE ESTATE INTERVIEW

Ben, I've heard you say that the purpose of a sales aid is to get the man's attention. If you get the man's attention you're better able to make a sale. Your tax tables and your probate charts certainly get a man's attention, and start him thinking as well. Do you use any other sales aids in your estate interview?

Occasionally, I'll take two unsigned checks out of my pocket and show it to the prospect. One check is payable to Internal Revenue Service for $100,000 and the other check is payable to my company for $300. I'll say:

"Some day you're going to sign one of these checks. Which one, Mr. Prospect?"

Sometimes I hand him the $100,000 check and ask him to sign it. Naturally, he hesitates. Then I hand him the check for $300.

"Just sign the little one," I say, "and I'll sign the big one."

36

HOW TO HANDLE MULTI-MILLION-DOLLAR ESTATE PROBLEMS

What puzzles me is that men with multi-million dollar estates don't know enough to get insurance protection. Don't they have advisors?

This man was a Senator. A very wealthy man. A large part of his assets was wrapped up in an oil company. You would think that such a man would have access to good counsel, wouldn't you? Working with attorneys, working with auditors all the time he should have good guidance, you'd think. But one day he died, and the taxes came to nine million dollars. And there wasn't any money. I wouldn't say he had good counsel, would you?

SENATOR ROBERT S. KERR
U.S. Senator, Oklahoma City, Oklahoma
Died January 1, 1963
Gross Estate Approximately $20,000,000

THE TULSA TRIBUNE   MARCH 31, 1964

$9.4 MILLION DUE

Taxes Will Take About Half of Kerr's Estate

From the State Capitol
Bureau of The Tribune

OKLAHOMA CITY—Federal and state inheritance taxes will take almost half of the late Sen. Robert S. Kerr's $20.8 milion estate, it developed today.

Executors of the estate have advised the county court $9.4 million in inheritance taxes are due Wednesday and it will be necessary to raise $6.1 million to pay the tax bill.

The executors, Dean A. McGee, president of Kerr-McGee Oil Industries Inc., and Robert S. Kerr Jr., asked for permission to borrow the money needed and pledge the assets of the estate as security.

LOANS OF $1.6 MILLION from the Liberty National Bank of Oklahoma City and of $4.5 million from the First National Bank of Chicago are planned.

In their petition, the executors assert that sale of Kerr-McGee stock—which makes up two-thirds of the estate—would depress the market and cause a substantial loss to the estate.

Largest single item in the estate of the senator, who died in Washington Jan. 1, 1963, of a heart attack, was block of 449,882 shares of stock in Kerr-McGee Oil Industries, Inc. valued at $14,472,703.

Kerr's will left his estate in trusts for the benefit of his wife and children.

Senator Robert S. Kerr's will was written in 1939 and was never up-dated to take advantage of the marital deduction provisions of the present Federal Estate Tax laws. While attorneys had prepared a revised will, the Senator apparently never took time to sign it.

The result is that Senator Kerr's estate, which means his widow and children, will have to pay almost $9,500,000 in Federal and State Estate Taxes alone, plus substantial administration expenses. The executors have already borrowed over $6,000,000 to pay these estate taxes, which were due April 1, 1964.

Proper estate planning could have saved this estate over $4,000,000.

© ESTATE RESEARCH CO.

SENATOR ROBERT S. KERR
United States Senator
Oklahoma City, Oklahoma

SETTLEMENT COSTS

Died January 1, 1963, at age 66

Gross Estate	$20,800,000
Total Costs	9,840,000
Net Estate	$10,960,000

Cash in Estate, $113,000.

Debts .... $Unknown (1)

Borne by Heirs

Admn. Expense	....
Attorney's Fee	220,000
Executor's Fee	220,000
Okla. Estate Tax and	
*Federal Estate Tax	9,400,000
TOTAL COSTS	**$9,840,000**

Debts Day Before Death

Debts Day Before Death

Debts Day After Death

(1) The exact gross estate has not been determined due to complexity of valuations. The executors petitioned the Probate Court for permission to borrow $6,100,000 from two banks to help pay estate taxes rather than sell shares of Kerr-McGee Oil Industries, Inc. stock (449,862 shares valued at $14,472,703) which would have depressed the market and caused substantial loss to the estate.

Under Will the widow was given a life estate in one-sixth of the estate left for her in trust. She renounced the Will and chose to take as a forced heir as if decedent died intestate, all as provided by Oklahoma law, thereby taking one-third of entire estate.

OVER 47% SHRINKAGE

*33 1/3% Marital Deduction

© Estate Research Company 1972, P.O. Box 2157, Castro Valley, California 94546

125

Where was the nine million dollars to come from? Who in the world with an estate of about twenty million, has around half of it lying around loose? Where can an estate get that kind of money without liquidating something? There was a lot of stock but the executors were concerned with depressing the value of the stock so much that the estate—everybody—would suffer, so they decided not to sell the stock. What did they do? They went to a bank, and luckily were able to borrow six million dollars. But they had to have nine million dollars. They were able to find the additional three million in cash.

The interest on the six million amounted to about $420,000 a year. The Senator was around the 60-year mark, and the premium on a policy would have been about $60 per thousand or about 6%. Six percent on six million dollars would have been about $360,000 per year. So by borrowing, the estate paid $420,000 not $360,000. And the estate had to pay the six million dollars back as well.

These things can happen, and they *do* happen.

*Had you been able to show
the Senator his problem he probably
would have solved it your way?*

Yes. Instead he solved his problem by postponing it.

*Could you give me a case history of a
man you got to before he postponed his
decision too long?*

Here's a case I'm actually working on now. I have a man who's spent all his lifetime becoming wealthy. Now he has an estate that runs into eight figures. The reason the estate grew that big is that this man has the ability to make money make money. He's still doing it. That means the money is not lying around in the form of dollars; it's wrapped up in something. Now someone's going to have to unwrap it when the man walks out and Uncle Sam walks in. The executors won't have a lot of time to do it; under the new tax bill they have only nine months. The executors may not be able to liquidate without a great loss, so I'm going to go back to see this 70-year-old man.

I think he needs roughly $4,000,000 to pay what has to be paid from an estate standpoint. I'm going to make up a check for $35,000 payable to New York Life; that represents a premium. I'm going to make up another check for $4,000,000; that represents a problem. The $4,000,000 check will be signed by New York Life and be made payable to his company.

I won't ask him to sign the $35,000 check. I'll ask his company to sign it. It won't even be a personal obligation on his shoulders. I'll ask *him* for nothing. I'll show the man that if his company doesn't sign that $35,000 monthly check, they'll have to borrow. They'll be signing a $35,000 interest check, and they'll still have to repay the $4,000,000.

Where's the company to get that $35,000 each month? There's a tremendous flow of cash going through big companies every month. Look at a company doing $12,000,000 in sales. That's a million a month flowing through that company. It isn't difficult for that company to sign a check for $1,000 a month, or $10,000 a month, or even $35,000 a month.

Suppose the man dies three years from now. The

company will have paid in roughly one million. It will collect four million, a gain of three million! And no income tax! The company would have to earn six million to duplicate that gain!

Using insurance to protect an estate
from falling apart seems so obvious that
it's hard to believe anybody could say,
"no" to you, Ben. But I'm sure it happens.
Could you tell me about a case when somebody
did say "no"—and how you handled it?

I have another case I'm working with now. He's a man about 70. I know him. I heard some months ago that his wife had died. When he lost her, he lost his right to what we call a "marital deduction," which is the right to transfer half of his estate to her without paying the tax. So there'll be a lot of tax when he walks out.

I called on him. But he didn't want life insurance. He had a three million dollar estate, but he didn't want life insurance. He could make more money with his money by putting it somewhere else, he said. He wouldn't talk to me or see me after that. Either he was on the phone, or he was at a meeting—there was always some excuse.

So I left him a little package. I gave it to him through his personal secretary. In the package was a tax table. Also a probate record and an actual illustration on a million dollar policy. I also put a little note that I had written to him in the package. What did the note say? Something along these lines:

"All your life you've made decisions. You've tried to make good ones. You've succeeded, and now you may have a very substantial estate. Here's another decision. It's a good one. Let us pay the tax. If you will give us the interest we will pay the tax. A million dollar policy costs 7% per year. Just 7%. Why do you want to throw a million dollars away? How long did it take you to earn a million dollars? You probably had to earn two million to keep a million. Mr. Jones, all your life, you've exercised good judgment. So why not now? My dollars cost pennies apiece. Yours will cost two dollars apiece. Why not use mine?"

Did this note get you in to see the man?

It will. He'll see me. He's a very shrewd business-man and if there's a chance to make a dollar to save a dollar he'll be very interested. We're talking about a million dollars. His money or my money. He can get my plan and I'll pay the million dollars. If he can't get my money, he'll pay the million dollars. "Mr. Jones, do you want to take a million dollars out of your estate? It's one-third of your lifetime— Don't you care?" When I see him, I'll close the sale.

37

THE ESTATE CASE ILLUSTRATION: IT LOOKS DOWN THE ROAD TO BIGGER SALES

> *Could you show me one or two typical illustrations to demonstrate the estate problem?*

Here are a couple of recent ones:

TODAY

FOR MR. & MRS. JOHN DOE

		JOHN DOE	MARY DOE	TOTAL TAX
ESTATE OF	$500,000			
MARITAL DEDUCTION	$250,000			
NET ESTATE		$250,000	$250,000	
1. Federal Tax		$32,800*	$23,800**	$ 56,600
2. State Inheritance Tax		24,000	7,000	31,000
3. Administration Costs (approx. 4%)		20,000	10,000	30,000
4. Miscellaneous Items		5,000	3,000	8,000
TOTAL		$81,800	$43,800	$125,600

*Assuming death in 1979.
**Assuming death in 1985.

TOTAL REQUIREMENT - $125,600

LOSS OF CREDIT FOR MARITAL DEDUCTION
WILL INCREASE TAX ON FIRST ESTATE

TOMORROW

FOR MR. & MRS. JOHN DOE

	JOHN DOE	MARY DOE	TOTAL TAX
ESTATE OF	$1,000,000		
MARITAL DEDUCTION	$500,000		
NET ESTATE	$500,000	$500,000	
1. Federal Tax	$117,800*	$108,800**	$226,600
2. State Inheritance Tax	55,000	24,000	79,000
3. Administration Costs (approx. 4%)	40,000	20,000	60,000
4. Miscellaneous Items	15,000	10,000	25,000
TOTAL	$227,800	$162,800	$390,600

*Assuming death in 1979.
**Assuming death in 1985.

TOTAL REQUIREMENT - $390,600

LOSS OF CREDIT FOR MARITAL DEDUCTION WILL INCREASE TAX ON FIRST ESTATE.

Are there any variations on
the estate illustrations, or
are they all very much alike?

I would say that they're all very much alike. The tax structure is pretty rigid. The illustrations are governed by the size of the estate.

I notice that in both the illus-
trations that you've shown me,
you're looking down the road.

If you project that the man's growing and if you project the rate of growth for another five years, another ten years, then his estate can double.

Suppose a man is 70 years old.
You won't be projecting that
estate much further, will you?

Life expectancy tables would give that man possibly ten more years.

And you project that far and calculate
that his estate will continue to grow until then?

Assuming it does, and taking a very conservative figure—just assume it'll grow 5%—10 years down the road, the estate has increased 50%.

So, then, every one of your illus-
trations will always be looking down the
road as far as the estate problem is concerned?

Yes, I might say:

"Mr. Smith, you're 40 and your company is now worth one hundred thousand dollars. Your company is going to grow, and when you're 50 it will be worth $200,000. When you're sixty it'll be worth $300,000. Your life expectancy is 32 years. When you're 72, your company will be worth a million. If you wait until then to guarantee the cash you'll have to pay Uncle Sam, it'll be too late. Because even if you could get up the premiums, their cost would be prohibitive. But you can do it now.

"You don't have any money now? Well, just take an option on it now. That's term insurance. Let's do this. Let's set up $50,000 in permanent coverage and an additional $100,000 in term coverage. If you wait, you may become completely uninsurable. If you wait and you *get* the policy, you won't pay less; you'll always pay more. Take a life insurance policy and study the costs: the sooner you buy, the better."

Here's another example:

A man 38. An estate of five million dollars. I'm looking down the road. At age 48, his estate is going to double. At age 58, it'll be five times what it is today. But *today,* he can buy dollars for 54 cents. You know what that will cost him at age *fifty-eight? Seventy-five* cents!

"So why not buy it now, Mr. Jones? You're better off buying it sooner than later."

38

SELLING THE MILLION DOLLAR POLICY

What I'm going to try to do for this month is create cases that range from one million to possibly eight million. What I'm going to try to do is arrange for a medical examination. I'll see the man and present his problem and tell him that, "I'd like to put it together and you take a look. All I need now is to make sure that you're insurable."

Are these cold cases or are they cases for clients that are already in your files?

Seventy-five percent of these cases are policyholders. As a rule, you can't go out from scratch and write a policy for a million dollars. There's something called "confidence"—the man has to buy a little piece of you. While he may not understand you completely, he must be sure in his mind that you're thinking of him. He senses that you're knowledgeable and that you know what you're doing, that you do have a solution. He knows you're not backing him into a corner for a decision. Never do that, because he'll not give you a decision, or he'll not give you the right one. So, "Let me put it together. . . ." Ask him for nothing—just time.

How do you sell a million dollar policy to someone not in your files?

I have a case I'm working on for someone in his mid-thirties. He is already a wealthy young man. We have a million dollar contract with a premium of only $2,000 a month. The $2,000 a month will be a corporate payment. For a corporation that runs into many millions, $2,000 a month isn't even petty cash; it isn't a load for the corporation.

The contract is guaranteed to make a million dollars. You know why? We have a very special rider attached to the contract which states, in essence, "We'll give *you back your money—and a million besides.*"

How can we do this?

"Because, Mr. Smith, as you pay in premiums you pile up cash. The rider in the contract adds enough term insurance to cover the cash. If you were paying $2,000 a month—that's $24,000 a year—twenty years later you've paid in roughly half a million dollars, and the cash value is half a million dollars. You wrap your car around a tree, or get on the wrong airplane, and something happens to you— what we do is first pay the cash value, which is about equal to the premium. It's a recovery of cost. You never put in the amount you're going to pay out. It has to make a million dollars."

So that's the package—a very simple package.

Ben, I would think you have many cases in your files where a man is growing. His estate isn't worth a million now, but he's growing—you can see that—and one day his estate taxes will come to a million. I'm sure you're looking down the road. How do you sell such a man?

If a man needs a million dollars or more when he dies, he *does* have a problem! I say to that man:

"How would you like to be a millionaire? Put me on your payroll for $100 a day—and the day you walk out, one million dollars walks in. *Plus* about seventy-five per cent of the amount you paid in. Let me put it together. . . ."

Or I might say:

"We've just put $1,000,000 into an escrow account and have written your name on it. If you'll put me on your payroll for $2,000 a month, someday I'll pay your company one million dollars. Your estate will have to pay $1,000,000 for the tax, but your company won't have to pay much for the $1,000,000. Let me put it together. . . ."

39

WHEN A MAN'S CORPORATION IS THE BULK OF THE ESTATE

How do you handle the estate problem when a man's corporation is the bulk of the estate?

I say to the man: "You could pull money out of your corporation, and give it to Uncle Sam, and maybe not wreck your company. It wouldn't break it, but it would bend it. You just cannot pull that kind of money out of a corporation without leaving a hole someplace.

"You know, there's an easier way of doing it. A man goes along and he works and he works and he works, and he makes money, and then he spends the money. And in a case like yours, you keep plowing it back into the corporation. Why? The corporation is growing. It's getting bigger: more land, more receivables, more inventory, more this, more that, more everything under the sun. And because you're doing this, it *is* getting bigger and bigger. After a while, it's the biggest thing you've got. And because it represents the bulk of your estate, it creates the estate problem.

"Even Uncle Sam recognized this and some years ago revised a section of the Revenue Code, and now the corporation can pay your tax. But the corporation had better have the money. So the insurance industry designed a contract that creates the cash.

"It's so simple. You do nothing. Your company sets up a special account and puts $10.00 a day in it. My company sets up a special account, and we put $100,000 in it. Some day we simply trade accounts. Let me put it together. . . ."

What I was trying to get him to buy was nothing but a Split Dollar Contract.

> *Did your client deduct the*
> *premium as a business expense*
> *or corporation expense?*

No. There is no way to deduct it.

> *There is not? You said it*
> *was a close corporation.*

There is no method of deducting the premiums. Not unless he picks it up as income. That's not what we're trying to do.

I see. The corporation does not place its coverage on him as part of his compensation?

That's right. If the corporation wants to buy a policy, pay the premium, but vest ownership of the policy in him, certainly. But he must pick up the premium as additional compensation.

See, what I'm trying to do is to get the corporation to buy a policy of $100,000. On whose life? On his life. They own it. They pay for it. They collect the proceeds. They do not deduct the premiums. But they do *not* pay tax on the proceeds; and I promise you the proceeds will exceed the premiums. Then, under Section 303, this man's executor can redeem enough of his stock, sell back enough of his stock to the corporation to pull this money back out. The executor can pull it out without tax consequence of any kind, and pay the entire cost of settling this man's estate.

There are a lot of variations you can get into in the Split Dollar Plan. There are a lot of things you can do. But basically I have in mind nothing but a very simple little contract owned by the corporation.

40

HOW TO SELL A PACKAGE THAT GUARANTEES COMPANY CONTINUITY

I say to a man:

"There's a price tag on everything. A man spends a lifetime making money, plowing it back into a successful corporation, becomes quite wealthy, worth a lot of money, and yet he has no money—that is, money in the form of dollars. To keep growing, you convert dollars into other assets. In other words, you lock them up. But someday you're going to have to unlock them; and if you're not here, it may become a liquidation. The other word for liquidation is quite

often—loss. You spend a lifetime accumulating assets. Someone will take them apart over night.

"If a man is willing to trade a lifetime for his estate
it should be worth keeping. It represents his life. A long,
long time ago, you got to the point where you were no longer
working for bread and butter. Yesterday you earned enough
money to buy two pairs of shoes, but you're only wearing one.
Why only one? You could have purchased two neckties, but
you are only wearing one. So what are you doing? You're
piling up something in the form of brick, stone, steel, land.
This is your estate. This is your life. And, you know, you
didn't build all this for the purpose of permitting it to fall
apart. You prize your company. There are a lot of people
depending on your company. I mean your family, and the
families of all the people you employ.

"Now let us put a floor beneath it. Sure, we can
drain your company of cash. *Do you think the company
could continue?* You're going to need some dollars, and I have
guaranteed dollars. They're guaranteed and they're discounted.
You never pay in the amount you pay out. Furthermore, the
gain is free of income tax. You're going to need some money.
Why don't you use my dollars? They cost pennies apiece. Let
me put the plan together and you take a look."

*What are the price tags on your
company continuity packages?*

They depend on the tax impact—the biggest factor
that I know of in the entire field of life insurance. The tax
impact creates the need for massive amounts of money. I
have a case pending now for $15,000,000! Why? It isn't for

the man. It's to keep together what he put together. It's to take care of tax impact on the estate.

"You'd like to be sure that your company goes on after you're no longer here. I'd like to show you that there is enough money to take care of your estate—without forcing the liquidation of estate assets."

41

A PACKAGE TO INSURE ONE YEAR'S PROFITS

*In close corporations—family held
corporations—the man usually wants
his son to carry on. Sometimes when
the son takes over, because of the son's
inexperience, it's more of a threat to
the company than the estate taxes. Is
there any way you can insure the company's
continuity in this case?*

Yes, those men who have the bulk of what they own
wrapped up in their company quite often want the company
to continue. Suppose they have a son. They want the son to
carry on. And yet they know, the day they walk out, problems
walk in. So tell a man:

"Here's a cushion, a cash cushion, for your boy to lean on. He's bound to make some mistakes along the way. You know, there are two kinds of mistakes: little ones and big ones. The little ones, the company can absorb. The big ones? They'll absorb the company. So, give your son something to lean on. Give him some time. Let's insure one year's profits. Give him a year's time to get his feet down solid and make the wheels go round."

What if the man tells you that he's going to deed his estate to his son? What would you tell the man, Ben?

I would say this:

"Mr. Jones, the government levies a tax on your right to make money. They call it income tax, and you are familiar with it because you pay it every year. The government *also levies a tax on your right to transfer what is left to your family*. You are not familiar with it, because you have never died. You cannot deed your entire estate to your son. You will deed it to the tax collector and your son. *And I promise you, the tax collector will come first and your son will come second.*

"Do you have lots of money? Is that money in your corporation? Now what little you do have, your executors will have to take out and give the tax collector. You have difficulty running your company even *with* money. Do you think your son can run it *without* money?"

You see, you can have a beautiful case when you pinpoint the problem. He is proud of his company. He wants it to go on. He wants it to continue. No man wants to work all his life and then feel that everything he's built up is falling apart. He has a boy, and he wants the boy to carry on. He would like the boy to pick it up where Pop drops it, and keep running with it. That's just human. That's normal. That's what we all want. But the tax structure won't let us do it. You can *not* disregard the tax structure. If you do, you work for what? For nothing.

42

*HOW TO
CREATE A
GUARANTEED
MARKET*

> *Suppose a man isn't interested in
> company continuity. Suppose he wants
> to sell in the event of his death. What
> do you do then, Ben?*

I'll give you an example. I get a D&B on the
XYZ Company. I study the picture. The Company's worth
about a million dollars. It looks like a one-man operation.
One man—he makes the wheels go round. And that's a problem in itself—the problem of the close corporation. And
you know what that problem is? The problem of a close corporation is that it's *closed*: the money that he puts in is *closed*

153

in, locked in—locked into land and machinery, into bricks and steel. A man spends his life putting money *in*—tell me, how is he going to get that money *out?* Particularly after he's gone? Because the day he stops, the company stops—and who wants the company then—at *any* price? And if it *is* sold, it's sold only for what the land and buildings and machinery will bring— and that's only a fraction of what the man put in; it's not the million dollars or so the Company is really worth.

And what happens to this man's widow? He's going to leave her *locked-in* to the company, but *locked-out* when it comes to cash. How is this man going to unlock the value in the Company—all the money he's put into that Company over the years? How is he going to unlock that million dollars so he can pass it on to his widow? You know, the widow is much better off with a million dollars in U.S. Bonds than a million dollars in bricks and machinery.

So this man has a problem—a million dollar problem.

The moment he walks out, he wants his widow bailed out. He wants to sell the company after he dies. But how can he be sure there's going to be a buyer? After all, it's a close corporation. *He's* the company. When he's gone, what's the company worth? And if there is a buyer, how can the man be sure the buyer will pay the price tag that this man puts on the company? And you can be sure that the price tag will be a big one. So when you look through this man's eyes, you see that his problem is a big one—a problem that might look to him like it could never be solved.

But why can't you *guarantee a market* for his company? It's simply an agreement worked out between two companies. When one man dies, the other company buys. And *you* guarantee the money with life insurance on the man's life. The company that buys is the beneficiary.

And don't forget, the company president who *buys,* pays for the company he buys with *discounted* dollars. Look what a wonderful thing life insurance is: The man who *buys* the company, buys it for pennies on the dollar. And yet the man who *sells* the company gets every dollar he writes on the price tag! So say to a man:

"Everybody will know that your widow will have to pay the tax, so it won't be possible for her to get a good price on anything that has to be sold. Let me show you how to protect your widow against bargain seekers. I will create a guaranteed market—a policy designed to convert bricks and steel into dollars, so your family ends up with dollars instead of frozen **assets.**"

> *Ben, you looked at the problem*
> *through the eyes of the man who*
> *wanted to sell. How about looking*
> *at it through the eyes of the man*
> *you'll have to convince to do the*
> *buying. Remember, it's this man*
> *who'll be paying the premiums.*
> *Just how would I*
> *go about convincing him?*

Ask yourself: what's this man's problem? *My competitor's put a one hundred thousand dollar price tag on his company. But that's too much for me. How can I buy it for less?* You say to the man, "How would you like to buy your competitor's company for pennies on a dollar?" Would he? You bet your life he would.

But don't stop there. Remember, this man is watching pennies. Say to the man:

"From a   four thousand dollar premium, three thousand dollars is plowed back into cash value. We keep only one thousand dollars a year and guarantee to pay one hundred thousand dollars someday. How many years would it take *you* to pay in the amount we pay out?"

It's a very simple package designed to create cash to buy a competitive business—a "purchase package."

43

HOW TO GUARANTEE STOCK REDEMPTION

*Suppose a man doesn't want to sell
his company—all he wants to be
sure of is that the company has the
money to redeem his stock when he walks
out. What can you do about that, Ben?*

Let's take a specific instance. I have a case. It's a large trucking company. Going over the D & B, I see it's a typical family company—father, son, and son-in-law. I find the party who started the company is getting on in years, and is probably no longer active. I can see a need for insurance to

pay estate tax to keep together what they've put together.
I can also see a need for cash to redeem stock.

Visualize what happens when the father dies. The
family doesn't want outsiders to buy the stock. What should
happen with the stock is that it should be redeemed, so that
it can remain closely held. The family would be willing to
redeem the stock if they had the money. But something has
to be done to pay the tax.

The problem here is this: the corporation must
have insurance on the father to redeem his stock. They need
estate dollars. The widow will be better off with cash than
she will with a share of the stock from which she can get
little or no income. We need insurance on the boys to redeem
the stock. The family will be better off with the cash.

The stock's got a basic value of two million dollars. The father owns 40% and the rest is broken up among
the children—12%, 12%, 12%, 12%, and 12%. Now if the
stock of the father is redeemed, then the equity of the children
remains equal. The father intended it to be equal, or he
wouldn't have given them equal amounts. Let's keep it that
way.

Let's not have the mother dependent on what may
happen once her husband's gone; make her independent. See
that there's enough cash to bail out the estate, enough cash
to redeem the stock. Let her have her independence. Let
the children go on, and do with the company what they are
capable of doing.

This is one of my cold prospects. I haven't made
the call yet. Look how much time you spend getting ready
to get ready. You finally get to the point where you know as
much about the company as the prospect knows. When you

make the call, you can hit home quickly, simply; show the tax impact.

Don't most companies already have
corporate insurance to guarantee
stock redemption?

You'll find very few companies that have corporate insurance. And any insurance they have, they bought years ago; it's outmoded. Companies grow and continue to grow. So you can find a need for more insurance. You underwrite the problems of today, then go a little farther, and underwrite tomorrow—because the company will get bigger. Say to the prospect:

"Have you thought about a public offering of your stock? What about a private offering? It's much simpler, and it will also get your dollars out. It's simply an agreement between you and your company, with my company furnishing the money."

Ben, you've been talking about
close corporations. How shall I
approach the problem of stock
redemption in a public corporation?

The key to insurance in a public corporation is this: a substantial stockholder still needs estate tax dollars. In all probability, his stock will need to be sold. Set up a guaranteed market for his stock through his company, and your company will guarantee the cash. Say to the man:

"You will have the certainty of a guaranteed market with guaranteed dollars—plus your company gets your stock at a discount."

44

PARTNERSHIP: SEE-SAW INSURANCE

*You've shown me many ways to use
insurance to keep a close corporation
going after a man's death—and
helping the widow and the family. You
have a package which applies to partnerships—can you tell me how that works?*

Did you ever hear of see-saw insurance? It's a
very simple expression for what some people call business
insurance. There are two men in business and they're on a
see-saw. They balance each other.

But, can you imagine one man see-sawing if the
other man gets off? If one man gets off, the other man falls
off. He can't see-saw alone.

Here again, I'll walk in and say: "Look, put me on your payroll for $10 a day, or $10 a week, or whatever. And the day he falls off, I'll bring you enough money to buy out his business interest."

Why does he want to buy out his partner's interest? You know, when a partner walks out, his widow walks in. What does she know about the business? The surviving partner doesn't want to conduct his business with his partner's widow. If the business is to continue, the surviving partner will want to buy out the widow.

But has he got the cash? His business is a business like any other business—it's stones and steel—it's *not* liquid assets. He just can't liquidate half the business without destroying the whole business. If you and I had a partnership worth two hundred thousand dollars, and we owned it equally, and one of us dies—do you think the other one of us could just cut the company in half and pull out the hundred thousand? *You* could not. *I* could not. So there's a problem: *How is a partner to get the cash to buy out the widow without destroying the company?*

Life insurance can easily solve that problem. It's simple. The partners insure each other. Each is the other's beneficiary. And there's an agreement to use the money to buy out the deceased partner's widow. So everybody's happy— the remaining partner *and* the widow. Tell me, isn't she much better off with her money no longer exposed to risk? Isn't she better off when her husband walks out to have her money walk in? Say to a man:

"You know, a partnership is like a see-saw: when one partner gets off, the other partner falls off. Here's a plan to buy out your partner—for pennies on the dollar. When one dies, the other buys. Let me show it to you."

*Don't you find many partnerships
already have agreements to buy each other
out in the event of one partner's death?*

Yes. It's an agreement that if you die, I buy. All
your interest is offered for sale. I have first right to buy. But I
better have the money. I've seen binding agreements: If you
die, I must buy. Yet I won't have the money. What good is
the agreement? It's an obligation. I've got to buy. But I
don't have the money. Maybe I can borrow it. Maybe I can't.
Say to a man:

"This is a plan designed to create cash for your
partner's half of the business. You set aside $300 a month.
If nothing happens, we will give you back your money. If
something happens, we will give you back your money, and
his share besides. Let me put it together. . . ."

*Suppose one of the partners is
appreciably older, how do you handle
that situation?*

In case of a cross purchase with the younger partner
paying higher premium for the older partner, say to the younger
partner, "You pay more but we pay sooner."

45

ONE POLICY
FOR THE
TAX COLLECTOR,
ANOTHER POLICY
FOR YOUR FAMILY

*You've been telling me, Ben, how
insurance can help a company from
falling apart. But what about the
widow and the children? What can
I do about the man's family?*

The man's family needs to go on living. Is there a
source of income? A life insurance contract has options that
are *designed* to provide an income. What you should do is
make sure that there will be a livable lifetime income for the
family.

165

For example: The man's been earning $2,000 a month. The family can live on $1,500 a month. Add an extra $500 in reserve, if the widow needs extra money for emergencies, for opportunities, for gifts to grandchildren—whatever she needs it for. If she doesn't use the extra money, there'll be cash to absorb the cash impact on *her* estate.

In handling a close corporation case, in the beginning what you do is the emergency work—what you do is create the cash for what has to be paid. You know what has to be paid? The day I walk out creditors walk in. You know who they are? My banker walked in. I made a promise to pay him some money. He wants some money. The IRS walked in. These debts must come first. But along with showing a man how these debts can be paid, tell him: "Here's an income for your family."

Explain to the man: "Your widow has no right to expect your company to pay her an income. Is she performing a service? What service: Can she step in your shoes and do what you've been doing? Will she be eligible to take out salary the way you've been taking it out? No. She owns pieces of paper. They pay no dividend. What will she do with it?"

Tell the man that there should be an income and a personal policy—even a split dollar policy—with the corporation paying the bulk of the premium. "There is a plan by which the corporation pays the premium. You have a very minor cost. Yet, the bulk of the proceeds go to your family."

Give the man, "One policy for the tax collector, and one policy for your family."

Of course, you can also give him a policy for his banker, and so on.

46

THE SALARY CONTINUATION PACKAGE

Can't you also use options, Ben,
to protect the widow?

Yes, you can build packages out of options.

"Mr. Jones, how would you like your widow to have three thousand dollars a month for life?"

By taking advantage of an option, you can arrange that, can't you? Three thousand dollars a month—that's the man's salary. So you can show the man that you have an

idea how his widow can continue to receive his salary even
after he's gone.

What do I call this package? It's my *salary continuation package.*

47

A PACKAGE
TO INSURE
COMPANY CREDIT

Ben, a man might say, "I need a large
sum of money to keep my company going
while I'm alive, so my company can
progress, move ahead. But how can I
guarantee the bank that my company
will be able to pay it back in case
something happens to me?"

Every man who runs a closely held business has
this kind of problem. A bank won't let his company borrow
money unless *he* promises to pay it back—because, after all,
he's the company. But how can he keep his promise if he

MILLION DOLLAR POLICY

JOHN DOE

THIS IS YOUR NET COST

THIS IS YOUR INSURANCE RETURN

End Of Year	Annual Premium	Increase In Cash Value	THIS IS YOUR NET COST	Face Value +	Accumulated Cash Value +	Dividend Account* =	Total Death Benefit
1)		—	[$23,605]		—	—	$1,000,000
2)		$ 18,800	[5,605]		18,000	$ 1,510	1,019,510
3)		20,000	[3,605]		38,000	4,560	1,042,560
4)		21,000	[2,605]		59,000	9,060	1,068,060
5)	$ 23,605	21,000	[2,605]	$1,000,000	80,000	15,230	1,095,230
6)		22,000	[1,605]		102,000	22,730	1,124,730
7)		22,000	[1,605]	TAX-FREE	124,000	31,560	1,155,560
8)		22,000	[1,605]		146,000	41,580	1,187,580
9)		23,000	[605]		169,000	52,680	1,221,680
10)		24,000	[-395]		193,000	64,800	1,257,800
TOTAL	$236,050	$193,000	[$43,050]				
AVERAGE	$ 23,605	$ 19,300	[$ 4,305]				

CASH VALUE OF DIVIDEND ACCOUNT
AFTER 10 YEARS IS $32,790

*Dividend account is paid-up additions and figures shown represent face amount of paid-up insurance.
Dividends are based on current illustrations and are not guarantees of future dividend results.

170

runs out of time? Where's the money to come from? When a man borrows, it's because he needs it. If he needs it, he spends it. He doesn't have any money. And if he runs out of time, how's the bank going to get its money back? You know something?—the bank is not going to let him have that money unless the bank is *sure* he can keep his promise.

Now life insurance can solve that problem. Life insurance puts a floor under time. Say to a man:

"Sooner or later, you're going to need more money from the bank. Your company is growing; you're going to need more cash to keep it growing. But will the bank give you the credit line you need unless you can guarantee the money in case something happens to you? Here's an idea: *a special contract* that insures corporate credit. Let me show it to you. . . ."

Here's an illustration on a man, aged forty, for one million dollars.

Why does this man need a million dollars? He needs it because he's a one-man corporation, and he's growing, and he needs money with which to grow. So he goes to banks to ask for money, and the banks want to know:

"If we lend you this money, are you going to pay it back? We have confidence that you'll pay it back—as long as you're here. But what happens if you wrap your car around a tree? We don't want to run your company. We're in the banking business. We don't want your company. We want the million dollars."

So I say to my prospect:

"With the stroke of a pen, I can create that million dollars for you. The day you walk out, a million dollars walks in.

"Look at the illustration. If you should die ten years from now, your corporation will have put $236,050 in this policy. You know what my company will do?

"We'll give you back the total cash value—which is $225,790—and what will we keep? The difference, which is roughly $10,000. And for the $10,000, do you know what I'll do? I'll come in personally and bring a check for one million dollars tax-free.

"Now, tell me—suppose you kept the $10,000— where would you invest it to run it up to a million?"

It's a simple illustration, but it's graphic, exciting, effective.

48

HOW TO WORK
ALONG WITH
THE BANKS
TO INCREASE
YOUR VOLUME

Do you ever help a man get a
loan by working along with a
bank and setting up the insurance?

If you present a good idea to a bank, then it'll
loan you the money. But the bank can't guarantee the time.
When a bank makes a loan to a man, it's really making a
loan based on confidence in a man and what he's going to

do with the money. The bank knows he's going to spend the money. The money will lose its identity; it'll become brick, stone, steel—everything except dollars. Now if the man has enough time, he'll make his plan work out. He'll keep his commitments and he'll repay his loan. If the man walks out, the bank doesn't want to be in a position of liquidating his company. The bank wants to be sure to get its money back. That's where I can work along with my client and the bank.

I have a case: He's got a million dollars in insurance. He doesn't need anymore. He doesn't want any more. He called me. He said, "I have a chance to buy a new company. I need $750,000. Where can I get that much money? You've been telling me about a bank in Youngstown that might be receptive. The new plant will be in Youngstown."

I set up an appointment between the banker and myself and this party. He needs money, and the bank is looking for a new customer—and if the deal looks good to them, they'll make the loan. If they make the loan, he needs time to pay it back. So I write $750,000 to cover it.

You know something?—when you write any policy payable to a company, you tend to make the company worth a little more money. Now, if you and I owned the ABC company equally, and if I died—somehow, someone would have to come up with enough money to pay for my stock. The bank loaned the company $750,000 and the life insurance policy paid it back. Suddenly the company is worth $750,000 more. Now my stocks are worth $375,000 more. We'll need some more insurance. It grows, and it grows. It never stops.

Does a bank ever pay
premiums on the policy?

Should there be a keyman policy assigned to the bank, quite often the bank will advance the money to pay the premiums for the policy as part of the loan. This is a very small price to pay for insuring the loan.

Keep in mind that, other than the first premium, the bulk of everything paid in simply piles up—becomes cash value. Show your banks how a contract creates cash. Show them that there's usually a tremendous gain to the corporation, and there's no income tax. It's a tax-free addition to corporate surplus.

Cultivate your banks. It's a new frontier of creative selling.

49

HOW TO SELL KEYMAN INSURANCE

*How about keyman insurance
—doesn't that create com-
pany credit?*

Keymen create corporate credit. Sometimes corporations find themselves locked up and locked out. This happens when a keyman dies unless he's insured.

*What's your approach when
talking to a keyman?*

177

Ask him, "Did you ever take a vacation? Ever go away for a couple of weeks?"

He'll say, "Yes."

"Any problems?"

He'll say, "No."

"Could you take a month off?"

He'll say, "Yes."

"Could you take a year off?"

Maybe he'll hesitate a little while. Maybe there'd be some problems if he took a year off.

Then tell him:

"You know, Mr. Jones, no man has a lease on life. One of these days you're going to walk out the door and you're *never* coming back. You think that would have a bearing on corporate credit? Corporate credit is very important to the continuity of your company and all the people depending on it, including your family. There's the telephone. Why don't you call your banker. Call your banker and ask this question: 'If you walked out and would never come back, and a short time later the tax collector walked in and took all the money, would it have any bearing on your company's credit line? Or would the bank be willing to go along as they have in the past?' "

I have never yet found a man brave enough to make that call.

Say to that man, "Do you think your bank will extend the same credit line to the man who takes your place?"

What's your approach when
you're talking to the head
of a company about other keymen?

"Mr. Jones, your accountant even puts a box of stationery on your balance sheet, but ignores the man who makes your company a million dollars. While no man is indispensable, neither is your equipment, nor your building—and yet the equipment and building are insured, because you can't get a loan without insuring them.

"Yet machines and buildings don't make money. Only management—keymen—make money. When you lose a keyman you lose money. Keymen should be insured to indemnify the company.

"Your keyman is a money-making machine. With him here, there is a man at work. With him gone, it would simply be *money* at work. The contrast would be tremendous.

"Compare the earnings on money with the earnings of a keyman. One hundred thousand dollars will earn $5,000 a year. The same amount wrapped up in a company operated by a keyman may earn $20,000 to $50,000. The value of a keyman is many times the value of money.

"The ability of keymen means the difference between profit and loss. Insuring your keymen means insuring profits. The keymen are worth what you insure them for, and should be insured for what they are worth. My company

offers a policy that costs four cents per dollar, but returns
the dollar plus three cents out of every four.

"I'm not saying that a man is indispensable. I'm only
saying that the loss of a keyman can create problems.

"You've got a good many men working for you.
Why don't you hire one more. Me. Put me on your payroll.
Ten dollars a day. Set up a special account for me and put
$10 a day in it, and I'll set up a special account for you, and
put $100,000 in it! You know, it's going to take a long long
time for you to put in what you're someday going to take out.
Suppose I put it together and you take a look?"

When you sell keyman insurance,
do you look down the road?

You plan on living, don't you? No one plans on
dying. Not today. Maybe tomorrow, but not today. So when
I prepare my illustrations, I look down the road because
tomorrow is coming.

"And, Mr. Jones, if you don't want to go all the
way with a permanent block of insurance today, take an
option—buy a term policy—insure your insurability—at least
do that. And when the time comes—look, and exercise your
option."

50

THE BONUS POLICY

I had this keyman case. I walked into this closely held family company and found a man in his 50's who had been running pretty hard. The company represented the bulk of everything he owned in the world. It was growing and expanding. He was very proud of it. He wanted the company and the company name to be carried on by his son. His son was still a boy, not yet mature enough to step into his father's shoes. But the father had built a management team; and this team, if it could be locked in, could carry the company until the boy was mature enough to take over.

I said to this man:

"The biggest assets you have are these key people, and yet how can you be sure—if you get on the wrong airplane or in the wrong car, and one day you are gone—how can you be sure that these men will continue carrying your company on for the benefit of your family? Don't you think you should try to lock them in, or tie them up, in some manner? Don't you think you should give them a little something more, so they'll be a little more likely to stay instead of walking away?

"We have a special plan for special people. We call it a split dollar policy. It's an arrangement whereby these men receive benefits over and above the salary they're receiving now. Tell a keyman: 'Look, Joe, if something happens to you, I'm going to pay off the mortgage on your home, and I'm going to educate your children. This is all free. It won't cost you a penny.' "

Then I say to the man: "Over and above what it will do for the keymen, let me tell you what it will do for you. It will pay your company $100,000 to indemnify for the loss of a keyman. It'll return to your company all premiums you've paid. Suppose I put it together and you take a look?"

I call it the *Bonus Policy*. It's simply a block of whole life.

What was the size of the policy?

In this case, I wrote two policies, each for $300,000. The keymen are tickled to death. The man who owns the company is very happy.

CONTRIBUTORY SPLIT-DOLLAR ILLUSTRATION
DIVIDENDS APPLIED TO PURCHASE ONE-YEAR TERM INSURANCE AND
ANY BALANCE TO PURCHASE PAID-UP ADDITIONS

JOHN DOE — $100,000   BONUS POLICY   Age 40-M

PLAN — WHOLE LIFE   FACE AMOUNT — $100,000   ANNUAL PREMIUM — $2,383.00

Year	Total Cash Value End of Year*	Yearly Premium Paid By Employer	Yearly Premium Paid By Insured	Death Benefit to Insured's Employer	Death Benefit to Insured's Beneficiary	Approx. Economic Benefit to Insured
	(1)	(2)	(3)	(4)	(5)	(6)
1		$2,061	$322	$ 2,061	$ 97,939	$ 111
2	$ 1,873	2,061	322	4,122	95,878	132
3	4,008	2,061	322	6,184	97,767	169
4	6,314	2,061	322	8,245	98,111	204
5	8,731	2,061	322	10,306	98,600	243
6	11,338	2,061	322	12,367	99,414	289
7	14,037	2,061	322	14,428	100,378	340
8	16,837	2,061	322	16,489	101,490	398
9	19,840	2,061	322	19,031	102,357	458
10	23,039	2,061	322	22,108	102,913	524
11	26,141	2,383		25,077	103,493	918
12	29,353	2,383		28,146	104,071	997
13	32,668	2,383		31,319	104,637	1,084
14	36,184	2,383		34,689	105,684	1,185
15	39,910	2,383		38,252	106,403	1,293
16	43,635	2,383		41,819	107,075	1,410
17	47,663	2,383		45,674	107,697	1,539
18	51,674	2,383		49,523	108,296	1,680
19	55,974	2,383		53,642	108,876	1,834
20	60,257	2,383		57,739	109,359	2,003
At 62	68,732	2,383		65,493	110,395	2,396
At 65	81,344	2,383		77,621	111,906	3,142

IN 20 YEARS:
INSURED'S COST - $3,220 FOR $100,000 AND MORE OF INSURANCE.

(Dividends are based on current illustrations and are not guarantees or promises of future dividend results.)

**CONTRIBUTORY SPLIT-DOLLAR ILLUSTRATION
DIVIDENDS APPLIED TO PURCHASE ONE-YEAR TERM INSURANCE AND
ANY BALANCE TO PURCHASE PAID-UP ADDITIONS**

JOHN DOE — $100,000   BONUS POLICY   Age 40-M

PLAN — WHOLE LIFE   FACE AMOUNT — $100,000   ANNUAL PREMIUM — $2,383.00

Year	Guaranteed Cash Value End Year	Dividend End of Prior Year	One-Year Term Insurance Amount	One-Year Term Insurance Cost	Total Paid-Up Additions Beginning Of Year	Dividend Values End Year	Total Death Benefit
	(7)	(8)	(9)	(10)	(11)	(12)	(13)
1							$100,000
2	$ 1,800					$ 73	100,000
3	3,800	$ 73	$ 3,800	$ 14	$ 151	208	103,951
4	5,900	147	5,900	24	456	414	106,356
5	8,000	223	8,000	35	906	731	108,906
6	10,200	340	10,200	49	1,581	1,138	111,781
7	12,400	432	12,400	65	2,406	1,637	114,806
8	14,600	531	14,600	83	3,379	2,237	117,979
9	16,900	632	16,900	106	4,488	2,940	121,388
10	19,300	737	19,300	132	5,721	3,739	125,021
11	21,500	844	21,500	162	7,070	4,641	128,570
12	23,700	951	23,700	196	8,517	5,653	132,217
13	25,900	1,063	25,900	234	10,056	6,768	135,956
14	28,200	1,177	28,200	279	11,673	7,984	140,373
15	30,600	1,295	30,600	332	13,355	9,310	144,655
16	32,900	1,417	32,900	391	15,094	10,735	148,894
17	35,400	1,542	35,400	461	16,871	12,263	153,371
18	37,800	1,668	37,800	539	18,669	13,874	157,819
19	40,400	1,795	40,400	632	20,468	15,574	162,518
20	42,900	1,922	42,900	735	22,248	17,357	167,098
At 62	46,900	2,804	46,900	966	26,638	21,832	175,888
At 65	52,600	3,232	52,600	1,423	34,277	28,744	189,527

PREMIUM RATES — STANDARD RISK BASIS

ANNUAL PREMIUM

$100,00 WHOLE LIFE $2,383.00

(Dividends are based on current illustrations and are not guarantees or promises of future dividend results.)

51

HOW TO CREATE A SALE BY SWITCHING TO A YOUNGER KEYMAN

Ben, a lot of us have cases where we insure a keyman to back up a corporate credit line, and the insurance is assigned to a bank, and as the years go by, the keyman grows older, and a young man in the company becomes the real keyman, and takes over the drive of the company. What do you do about it?

I had such a case.

I went up to the older man and I said, "You know, the younger man seems to have become very active in your company. I imagine he could pretty much run it now, couldn't he?"

The older man said, "Certainly he could. I just sort of keep my finger on it now, but Bill is really running it. I think he could almost run it on his own."

I said, "You know, Ray, we locked up a big chunk of your corporate insurance when we assigned it to the bank. If we could persuade the bank that continuity for the company is built around Bill—ask the bank to let us substitute some insurance on Bill, and release some of the coverage on you—it might be well worthwhile."

That's exactly what we did. I approached the bank. I told the bankers that the young man, not the old man, is the keyman. Wouldn't they be better off actually in having substantial insurance on the new keyman, and release some of the insurance on the older man? They said they'd be willing to do this.

The man who owned the company was tickled to death to get his insurance back. We released the insurance on the older man and substituted insurance on the younger keyman.

52

A SPECIAL CONTRACT FOR THE MAN WHO HAS TOO MUCH MONEY

How can a man have too much money, Ben?

A man runs, runs, and runs, and after a while he has his business on a pretty good basis, with all the working capital he needs. He begins to pile up dollars—the kind of dollars he needs for inventory or for a new addition to the building—surplus dollars. Section 531 of the Internal Revenue Code is designed to prevent what Uncle Sam calls unreasonable accumulation of surplus. What is unreasonable? "The surplus money is needed to run the business," the man argues.

Well, prove it! The money's not wrapped up in the business. He's not using it. It's cash in a checkbook—in a certificate of deposit, or in commercial paper. It's not in the business. It's surplus.

The government states that you're allowed to accumulate up to $100,000. When you go over that, red flags go up. The IRS takes a look and says: "Mr. Jones, you can't do this. But you did do it. So there's an extra tax. The tax instead of being 50% is going to be 77%. It could go up to 88%. You made it, but you can't keep it."

It's called unreasonable accumulation—too much money. The money isn't the man's who earned it. It belongs to Uncle Sam. And Uncle Sam's going to take it. Not only is he going to take it, but he's going to penalize the man for not having given it to him sooner.

Is there a legal way by which
a man can avoid this tremendous
tax impact?

The man in business makes business decisions every day, and one of the decisions that he makes is the one that represents security for the company, continuity for the company. Most men looking down the road realize that no one has a lease on life. "Some day something will happen to me. Maybe sooner if I get on the wrong airplane." Say to this man:

"You know, there's another section of the Internal Revenue Code, Section 303, that's designed to really help people like you. The bulk of your estate is not in your pocket; it's in the company. The government realizes that it's not possible to get money out of that corporation without creating a big hole. But the government wants its money. The tax impact on the estate is creating your problem. A good corporate decision on your part is to make sure that the money the government will some day ask your family for will be available without the liquidation of assets.

"You know, when I find out your company has to be sold under forced liquidation, I'm going to be buying it. You know why? Because I'm not going to pay for it. I'm going to 'steal' it. I'm going to get it for nothing, or as close to nothing as possible. That's what you would do with *my* company. So, a good decision on your part would be to do what has to be done.

"Therefore, there should be a big big bulk of keyman coverage on you—money that walks in when you walk out. The coverage is not designed to make anybody money; it's just designed to keep together what you've put together. It's a good decision to buy those dollars for pennies apiece. If you're insurable, my company will put into escrow the million dollars that the government is going to ask for. If you don't let my company do it, then your family will have to do it. Let me put it together. . . ."

What I'm saying is that this man has too much money and he must invest it as outlined in keyman insurance. This would not be considered unreasonable, because the government wouldn't design a code that permits stock redemption; the government knows there has to be money with which to redeem the stock. So, the government designs 531 to prevent too much money, and it designs 303 to permit stock redemptions.

The contract I've outlined will accumulate a lot of money. But wouldn't it be difficult to say it was an unreasonable accumulation? In all the years that have gone by, there have been many companies that have had a 531 problem, but there's yet to be a case where life insurance was involved that went to litigation.

53

USE IT
OR LOSE IT:
THAT'S THE WAY
IT WORKS WITH
THE FEDERAL
GIFT TAX
EXCLUSION

*While we're on the subject of tax
impact, can you tell me how you use
gifts to help a man lessen that impact?*

Use it or lose it. When you have the background on
that statement—use it or lose it—you'll understand. Use *what?*
Or lose *what?*

Use it. The government levies a tax on your right to make money. They call it income tax. The government levies a tax on your right to transfer what's left to your family. They call that estate tax. But, the government also gives you a right—the right to make transfers of money free of tax. The government calls this your gift tax exemption. You can make a gift to any one person each year of up to $3,000. Any time during the year—but *only* during the year.

Or lose it. Gift tax exemptions lapse each year on December 31st. Either you use them or lose them. Costs you nothing to use them. Costs you a lot if you don't. The gift exemption—use it or lose it!

The gift tax exemption renews the following year. But if you didn't use it for last year, you lost it. What does it cost to lose it? Let's see:

You'd like to make a gift of $3,000. To whom? Let's say to your son. And under the terms of your will it will be subject to estate tax. Using the right to make the gift *now*, you give him $3,000 on which you pay no tax. And $3,000 out of your estate may save a thousand dollars. You can save more than you can earn. Where can you put a dollar that will earn 30%? I know where you can put a dollar where it will *save* 30%. Because the tax on the top dollar in the estate tax will be 30%.

Will you show me how you use the Federal gift tax exclusion to sell insurance?

I had this case.

DIVIDEND ADDITIONS STATEMENT
GIFT POLICY

Age 5-M **Endowment At Age 65 - $317,164 Face Amount** **Annual Premium $3,000**

Year	Guaranteed Cash Value	Cash Value of Paid-Up Additions End Year	Increase In Total Cash Value	Total Cash Value	Total Death Benefit Beginning Year	Total Paid-Up Insurance Available	Cash Value of Paid-Up Insurance At Age 65
1					$ 317,164		
2	$ 634	$ 159	$ 793	$ 793	317,164	$ 3,652	$ 15,006
3	3,489	373	3,069	3,862	317,895	17,189	69,842
4	6,660	649	3,447	7,309	318,823	31,409	126,281
5	9,832	1,045	3,568	10,877	319,951	45,121	178,679
6	13,321	1,517	3,960	14,838	321,489	59,403	231,665
7	16,810	2,083	4,055	18,893	323,232	72,992	280,317
8	20,299	2,745	4,152	23,044	325,206	85,909	324,864
9	24,104	3,496	4,556	27,600	327,375	99,285	369,691
10	27,910	4,370	4,679	32,280	329,741	112,047	410,836
11	31,399	5,401	4,521	36,800	332,292	123,259	444,996
12	34,888	6,639	4,727	41,527	335,233	134,214	476,990
13	38,377	8,088	4,938	46,465	338,587	144,909	506,843
14	42,183	9,788	5,506	51,971	342,365	156,388	538,199
15	45,989	11,715	5,733	57,704	346,565	167,531	567,200
16	50,112	13,918	6,326	64,030	351,129	179,341	597,273
17	54,235	16,380	6,585	70,615	356,055	190,790	624,924
18	58,675	19,112	8,757	79,372	361,328	204,178	657,681
19	63,116	22,172	8,135	87,508	368,523	216,116	684,543
20	67,873	25,588	8,808	96,316	375,093	228,415	711,389
At 60	270,541	623,856	48,935	900,423	992,740	1,004,782	1,170,378
At 62	287,985	712,163	54,453	1,006,174	1,054,927	1,073,961	1,178,831
At 65	317,164	866,629	65,126	1,189,819	1,154,802		

AT AGE 65 TOTAL CASH OF $1,189,819 PROVIDES MONTHLY LIFE INCOME (AT LEAST 10 YEARS) OF $7,044 AT GUARANTEED RATE OR $10,108 AT CURRENT ANNUITY RATE.

USING ALL ACCRUED DIVIDEND VALUES POLICY COULD BE FULLY PAID-UP IN 26 YEARS. TOTAL CASH VALUE OF SUCH A PAID-UP POLICY AT AGE 65 — $881,845.

(Dividends are based on current illustrations and are not guarantees or promises of future dividend results.)

NO CURRENT TAX ON ACCUMULATING CASH VALUE.

Here was a man past 80 years of age and totally blind. He had been on disability income with New York Life and Prudential for about 30 years. The man had a family. This man had a great deal of courage and a real good mind. He had succeeded with the help of his children in building a successful business, a very substantial estate.

What man wants to run all his life piling up assets and then someday have a large part of those assets go down the drain? In this case, the man had no wife, no marital deduction. That meant Uncle Sam would take an even larger share of the estate.

It wasn't hard to show this man that it was too late, almost too late—and that he should begin thinking about, not piling up another dollar, but conserving the dollars he had exchanged a lifetime for.

Certainly, that man was not insurable. What could he do?

Between the children and grandchildren, there were ten beneficiaries. I set up ten policies, each with an exact $3,000 annual premium. He paid $30,000 in December and he paid $30,000 in January. He's going to pay $30,000 more in February, and we're going to get these policies paid up very quickly. I wrote ten policies, ranging between $30,000 and $40,000. Uncle Sam will subsidize a major part of the premiums through tax savings.

Year by year, the children and grandchildren are getting their share of the estate. What a wonderful gift for the children! They'll never forget who gave it to them.

Now there are other men like that—men with the same problem. I have a package for these men. It's called *Dollars for Your Grandchildren.*

•DOLLARS FOR YOUR GRANDCHILDREN•

	ANNUAL PREMIUM	ACCUMULATED FIGURES			INSURED FOR
YEARS		PREMIUMS	CASH VALUE	PAID-UP VALUE	
5)		$15,000	$10,000	$ 55,000)	
10)	$3,000	$30,000	$26,000	$124,000)	
15)		$45,000	$47,000	$196,000)	
21)		$63,000	$85,000	$296,735)	$296,735

S U M M A R Y

COST	CASH VALUE	PAID-UP VALUE
$63,000	$85,000	$296,735

(Dividend and interest estimates are based on current illustrations and are not guarantees or promises of future dividend results.)

Ben Feldman, C.L.U.

195

12/12/73

What grandfather doesn't want to help his grand-children? My *Grandchildren Package*—what's it for? To see to it that the children and grandchildren get their fair share of the estate.

Say to a man:

"Let's reduce the estate by making gifts to the people who are going to get it anyway—your grandchildren. Do it my way, without tax. It can be done as a gift to the grandchildren with your daughter as custodian. This means you still have effective control through her. The tax savings will pay for almost half of their education.

Ben, what would you say is the
key to this case?

The key to this case? Simply, keeping what you've got. Why spend a lifetime putting it together and then let it go down the drain?

Remember: There's a price tag on everything—doing something, and doing nothing. And quite often the price tag on doing nothing is much bigger than the price tag on doing something.

54

HOW TO HAVE CHARITABLE CONTRIBUTIONS GO ON FOREVER PAINLESSLY

Many companies make charitable contri-
butions as part of their tax program.
Certainly, these programs would be in
jeopardy with the death of a keyman in
a closely held corporation. Do you run
into this kind of problem? And, if so,
how do you solve it?

As you make your calls, from time to time you
find companies that are very, very charitable. These companies have been systematically and consistently making substantial gifts to charitable institutions in the community.

197

These gifts are often given with such regularity that they become a part of the charitable institution's budget. The institution depends upon them.

I ran into a closely held family company. It was started by the father, now deceased. It was carried on by a very able mother, also now deceased. It is being carried on by the children. One of the children is the keyman of the corporation.

The children had been given their own foundation, established in honor of their parents. The children had been giving the maximum corporate 5% to the foundation. The foundation had been distributing every penny of this money to charitable institutions in the community. These institutions had reached the point where they counted on this money. It was almost a must in their budgets. In addition, the children were giving their maximum personal contributions to other charitable institutions.

I pointed out to the children:

"You know what you're doing is wonderful. But you have set a precedent. These institutions depend on this money coming from you and your company. What will happen somewhere down the road if something happens to your keyman? It may be quite a load for you to keep on doing what you are doing, and it may be awkward to discontinue what you are doing. I have an idea. It can be very, very realistic. Let's see if we can put it together. . . ."

I wrote a $500,000 policy on the life of the keyman—the policy to be paid by the corporation. The proceeds of the policy were broken into two parts: one part, equal to the cash value, to be retained by the corporation; the other part, equal to the face value, to flow into their non-profit foundation.

The total premium was only $20,000 a year— $15,000 of which was retained through cash value, and $5,000 of which was a contribution. The cash value builds up on an average of $15,000 a year. There is no load on the corporation once the policy becomes a claim.

Some day $500,000, the face amount of the policy, will flow into a foundation. The $500,000, invested at only 5% will earn $25,000 a year forever. Insurance creates enough capital to make the charitable contributions painless and permanent.

55

HOW TO BUY A BIG CONTRACT

*Ben, you've been talking about
big policies. Do you have trouble
getting the underwriting?*

Ironic as it may sound, a big contract is harder to buy than it is to sell. Until a few years ago it was hard to buy $100,000. You could buy $10,000, $20,000, $50,000 but if you came into the office with $100,000, it was almost impossible to get the policy.

But you raised the sights of the
industry when you began writing
the million-dollar policy.
Now you're selling even bigger
ones. Those are the ones I want
to sell. Can I buy them?

The underwriting committee often doesn't want to give you a million dollar policy. They don't want that much risk. They don't even want a share of that much risk. Right now [this year] I have $30 million on the books paid, and $40 million I haven't yet been able to get. I have cases that have been examined, but every time the mail comes there's another request; we don't want this, we want this; we want another X-ray; we want another inspection report. They're reluctant. If you want a $10,000 policy, there are a hundred agents and a thousand companies that will get it for you tomorrow. Add a couple more zeros to the amount, and they don't want it.

Why are the underwriters
afraid to take the risk?

New York Life policies are incontestable after just one year. Many companies are after two years. Let's suppose you're holding a great big bundle of life insurance that's incontestable. Even if you committed suicide, even if you took an overdose of medication, we'd have to pay off. So you might do drastic things, things you wouldn't normally do. You know, you pick up the paper and read, "The man hit a bridge in broad daylight." No one can understand what happened. But he's dead.

*Does that mean the underwriters must
look into a man's character and activities
as well as his medical record?*

Yes. Let's suppose they pick up that you like other men's wives, they'll turn you down morally quicker than if they found out that you don't have a good sound financial program.

Say you're on a program of corporate acquisition. You acquire the XYZ company. It's losing a lot of money, say a million dollar loss. Your company is doing nothing but making money. You put those two companies together. You use your loss to cover your income tax. You acquire that company with Uncle Sam paying the bill. If you spread this kind of activity too thin, the underwriting committee will turn you down.

Underwriters will turn you down not only for medical reasons, but also just because they don't like what you're doing. They don't want large amounts of insurance unless there's a really good reason why the man needs it. I sometimes send an application into our home office and say I want half a million. They'll come back and say "What for?" I'll say, "He's in debt and owes half a million!" They'll say, "Why should we pay it?"

As a rule, to be able to get your life insured, you better measure up financially and morally as well as physically. Lead a good life!

You see, the big policy is harder to buy than it is to sell. You're doing a real service for that man if you can get it for him. Get everything put together, get him a thorough exam, then see what your Life underwriting committee will tell you. New York Life now will not hesitate on a hundred thousand dollar case but send down a million dollar case! I had a $4.4-million case recently. They not only didn't want it, they didn't want any part of it. They'd rather have ten people, each insured for a hundred thousand dollars, than one man insured for a million.

So sometimes you have to sell life underwriting as well as the prospect.

I submit all my cases to New York Life. If they turn a case down, and it's a "must" case, where I have to get insurance, then I'll look to other companies. Naturally, I try to favor my own company first, but if it doesn't work out, then I try somewhere else.

PART 3

56

HOW TO FIND THE FREEDOM TO SELL

> *If I had your volume, Ben,*
> *I'd never be able to set foot out of*
> *the office. How do you do it?*
> *How can I get that really important*
> *freedom—the freedom to sell?*

Get adequate office help and good equipment. Learn to delegate. Learn time control: establish priorities. Make use of procedures. Use the spread sheet and daily cards. Make up tomorrow's appointments today.

What do you mean by "delegate?"

I feel that you should invest money in yourself. You're in business. Do you know of a businessman who can operate a business without capital—without investing in himself? After a while you become a little more knowledgeable and when you do—delegate. Don't do what your secretary can do. When you find that you need a second secretary, get one. Don't spend your time doing what someone can do for one or two or three dollars an hour. Spend money! It will make you money! There's nothing quite for nothing.

Delegate to people and machines what they can do, so you can do what you do best.

Why are "priorities" important?

I found out a long, long time ago that you've got to do first things first. You've got to have a system of priorities. If you don't you'll get buried in detail.

Can you show me samples of your spread sheets and daily cards?

Here they are.

PLANNER-PAD

Your Success in Attaining Your Objective Is Primarily the Result of the Effective Use of Time — "THOSE WHO PLAN AHEAD . . . GET AHEAD"

PROSPECTS	PROSPECTS (continued)	EXAMINED	ISSUED	BINDERS	BROKERAGE

Planner-Pad, developed and copyrighted by H. Preston Smith, C.L.U., Denver, Co.

NEW NAMES SECURED TODAY

NAME	ADDRESS AND DATE OF BIRTH
1	
2	
3	
4	
5	

TO SEE TODAY

DATE _____

FORENOON

NAME	ADDRESS
1	
2	
3	
4	
5	
6	

AFTERNOON

1	
2	
3	
4	
5	
6	

EVENING

TELEPHONE

210

57

THE
SUCCESSFUL
SELLING ROUTINE

*Tell us a little bit
about your typical day.*

My office is just a stone's throw from my home. I get in about 8:00 A.M. About an hour later, one of the girls brings in all the mail. Someone else has gone through the mail, and I get only what I should be looking at.

I'll ask Barb to come in. She's the girl who does the correspondence. I'll get an idea and I'll say, "Put this down, put this down, put this down." She'll make up rough

memos. I'll write a number of letters. I don't have to dictate.
I'll just say, "Write a letter to so and so and tell him this."
She knows my thinking well enough. You see, I'm delegating.
I'm saving the time that I would have used if I had to dictate
the letter myself. She and I will spend maybe half an hour
together.

Then Marian comes in. She brings in a long list of
cases. She asks me which of these I must have. I'll say,
"I've got to have this one. I've got to have that one." I'll tell
her, "Make me up a Split Dollar on so and so." Or, "Make me
up a tax illustration." Or, "Make me up this or that, or something else." She has another girl who helps her. I'll spend
about 30 minutes with Marian.

I have a well-trained C.L.U. office administrator
who does my service work. He can do most of it himself, but
there are problem cases of all kinds. He'll run these by me.

By the way, it's this service man's job to make sure
a man gets examined. He'll call the man on the phone after
I've left, and he'll say, "Mr. Feldman asked me to call you.
I have an appointment set for Tuesday at 3:00 or one for
Friday at 4:00." The man will say: "What for? I haven't
bought any insurance!" My service man will say, "I don't
know, he just asked me to call you!" It may sound crazy, but
it works. Try it! It will work.

It's my administrator's job to follow through, and
get all the medical requirements fulfilled. The company may
want a statement from Dr. Brown and Dr. Smith, or they
may ask for an electrocardiograph or the Double Master's
Test, etc. That's *his* job. I don't want to nag my prospect. I
don't want to go near the man until I have something to sell.
When the policies finally come in, I decide what it is I want
to present and in what manner. It's up to me and I go back

to see him. Maybe he'll feel he's a busy man and I'm a busy man. Just a word on a piece of paper could mean so much. "Let's pin it down and then we'll have 30-60 days to work with your lawyer." I'll say, three times out of four he'll go along—that's my ratio. I'll place three out of four cases.

I try to get out of the office before noon. I don't always, though, because there are what seems to be a million phone calls coming in. A lot of calls came in the day before. There's a little blackboard in back of my desk with the messages. At 8:00 in the morning I have a lot of phone calls rolling out, but most of the people aren't in and I leave word for them to call back. They do, and you know, that means another pair of hands!

It's a relief for me to get out of the office. I have a radio set-up built into my car for my office and my home. It isn't telephone, it's radio. If something does take place, if someone calls in, if something happens that makes it necessary to reach me, they *can* reach me. They just call me. Doesn't matter where I am, they can reach me at once.

I go along making calls on a list I've made up the night before. I carry a little card in my pocket with maybe eight or ten names on it—to place policies, to try to complete an exam, or to get an interview. I'll walk in, make notes. The recording machine in my car is an indispensable tool.

It goes on like this for the rest of the day. Much of my work is in a radius of about 40 miles from my home. About 7:00 or 7:30 P.M. I'll call my home and ask if anything took place that I should know about; if anyone called in, or if there are any messages from the office. If there's anything I can do about these messages, I do it.

I bring a briefcase of work home with me. By now I'm so hungry—because I never take time for lunch and never take time for dinner until I get home—that when I walk into the kitchen I have what I call a "take-back" sandwich. I make myself a great big sandwich, and "take it back" into my bedroom. While I undress, I eat my sandwich. I get out of my clothes and put on old clothes. After I eat dinner, I work for an hour or two getting ready for tomorrow—earmarking, getting up the proposals I want Marian to type up the next day, maybe running over the dictation and picking out the things that are most important—things that really are the keys to the cases.

My day runs from 8:00 in the morning until 8:00 at night, with a couple of more hours thrown in to get ready for tomorrow. You see, there's no half way. You either do it or you don't.

Now that doesn't mean I work all the time. When I get tired, I go fishing for two or three days. From my home, it's only a couple of hours by jet down into the Florida Keys, and I know a man down there who is part fish! He can really find them whether they're biting or not. I get way out in a little boat—away from everything, not a sound to bother me. It's kind of good to be away. But after a couple of days I feel better and I go back and go to work.

58

HOW TO GET IDEAS THAT PAY OFF

> *Ben, your success is based*
> *largely on your ideas. How*
> *can I get successful ideas of*
> *my own?*

No man has a corner on ideas. You're successful because you have listened to other successful people. Get inspiration from others.

You can also learn from your own experiences. In sales work, the biggest mistake is not to make any mistakes.

215

59

HOW TO BUILD SELF-CONFIDENCE

*You've told me the way you sell
successfully, but there's one thing
you haven't told me: Just how can
I feel confident enough to go out
and sell. What's your advice?*

Accept yourself; the ability to improve is dependent first of all upon accepting ourselves as we are now with our strong points and our weaknesses. Then always be engaged in some type of self-improvement.

Remember, progress is mental in origin. We know that thinking habits develop a self-hypnotic influence. The

217

subconscious operates on the basis of images, not words. That's why we first must supply the mental equivalent of what we wish to achieve. Today and every day, act in accordance with the mental picture you have of yourself—your self-image.

Your confidence in yourself is determined by your personal estimate of your ability to handle the situation. Self-confidence is based upon past success. Think back to identical or similar situations that you handled successfully.

Also, *look* successful at all times.

60

THE "MAGIC" FORMULA FOR SUCCESS

If you had to sum up your formula for success in a few sentences, what would you say?

My formula for success?

I don't know, other than I really believe, and I try to be realistic: nothing for nothing. Most people buy not because they believe, but because the salesman believes.

And something else that's very important. You know, I'm very happy to answer questions, but once in a while, there is somebody who wants a magic answer. "What's the 'magic formula' for success?" My magic formula has always been hard work.

61

FELDMANISMS AND POWER PHRASES

Editor's Note: Many of the following Feldmanisms and Power Phrases are extracted from this book. They are all yours to adopt or adapt, moulding them to your own inimitable style and delivery, just as the author has done through the years.

I sell discounted dollars . . . may I show you?

We simply create the cash to pay what "must" be paid rather than risk loans and liquidations.

221

Let's use insurance to . . . keep together what you put together.

Do you have anyone on your payroll earning $1,000 per day? . . . you are!

We are on the risk for one million dollars and would like to re-evaluate your life expectancy. Wouldn't you like to know?

Do you think the bank will extend the same credit line to the man who takes your place?

You know you are the biggest asset on the balance sheet. Why shouldn't you be insured for what you are worth?

Wouldn't corporate credit be improved if your keymen were insured?

Did you ever compare the return on money with the return on a keyman?

How much is your life worth? How much did you insure it for?

May I talk to you about the $200,000 I owe you?

Let's insure your standard of living for your family.

We sell contracts for time and money. We can't guarantee the time, but we can guarantee the money.

Expand your partner's insurance because the day he 'walks out' his wife may want her 'money out'.

We have a special policy designed to discount your tax. May I show it to you?

It's not feasible to carry in cash the amount of cash your estate will need. Better to do it with a tax policy.

Every man in a growing company has some unfinished business . . . such as a note at the bank.

When a man dies, a lot of problems come walking in the door.

Remember, as time goes by, men grow—and as they grow, quite often their problems grow. The need is greater. So the solution must be greater.

If you can't put aside 3% of the amount now . . . where would 100% come from later? Buy a little less . . . but begin now.

Make up two checks . . . one for the premium and one for the proceeds. Then just say . . . you sign the little one . . . I'll sign the big one.

Mr. Jones, you have a problem. No one has a lease on life and most men never die at the right time; there is no right time. Mr. Jones, the taxes must be paid from your estate—or for your estate. Let me pay it for your estate—with discounted dollars.

There's a price tag on everything. By doing nothing it will cost you dollars. By doing something it will cost you pennies.

A positive mental attitude, that more than anything else determines your success. If you decide you are going to feel wonderful, strong, excited—then you have the power to move mountains.

O.K., I'll come back in five years. But if you're not here, who shall I ask for?

The best prospect is a man with a problem—all kinds of assets, but no money.

As a rule, you will sell each year ten times the amount of insurance you own. Build your own program up to one hundred thousand dollars, and you'll be writing one million dollars a year.

Let me make sure you're as good on the inside as you look on the outside. Could be you've waited too long. As the years go by, a man pays a price for success. Mother nature makes us a little bit older. And older doesn't mean better. Let's see if you can qualify.

The start of a sale is the interview. But the start of the interview is getting a man's attention. Unless you get his attention, you'll go no place.

In the interview, logic isn't enough. Use logic and emotion. Get the man stirred up. There's nothing like a disturbing question to build a fire under a man.

Never back a man into a corner and make him make a decision. Don't push. Lead.

Yes, you're in wonderful shape now. But your doctor didn't tell you how you'll be ten years from now. You see, we're going to take a look at how long you're going to live. Don't you want to know?

Most people buy not because they believe, but because the salesman believes.

You've got a good many men working for you. Why don't you hire one more. Me. Put me on your payroll. Ten dollars a day. Set up a special account for me and put $10 a day in it, and I'll set up a special account for you, and put $100,000 in it! You know, it's going to take a long, long time for you to put in what you're someday going to take out. Suppose I put it together and you take a look.

Never underestimate your prospect's needs. When you underestimate his needs, you're not helping him. When you think small, you're actually hurting the man you should be helping.

How would you like to be a millionaire? Put me on your payroll for $100 a day—and the day you walk out, one million dollars walks in. Plus *about seventy-five per cent of the amount you paid in. Let me put it together . . . .*

You know, there are two kinds of mistakes: little ones and big ones. The little ones, the company can absorb. The big ones? They'll absorb the company.

The mistake a lot of us make, you see, is to look for extra *money. If you reach down in a man's pocket for his wallet, he'll break your arm.*

When you save money in a bank, that's an accumulation. But we create money for you. Who else can do that?

Doing nothing doesn't solve your problem; it only postpones it. You have a right to postpone it. But if you postpone solving your problem, you know who'll have to solve it? Your wife.

If you have trouble paying pennies on the dollar, do you think your family will have it easy paying what must be paid with full hundred-cent dollars?

Why do you want to run hard for 30 years and then have 15 years go down the drain? You know there's a price if you do something or you don't do something. Most estates, some day, fall apart—not because you did something wrong, but because you did nothing; that's what's wrong.